EMPLOYEE RELATIONS POLICY AND DECISION MAKING

Employee Relations Policy and Decision Making

A survey of manufacturing
companies carried out for
the Confederation of
British Industry

ARTHUR MARSH
*Senior Research Fellow
in Industrial Relations at
St. Edmund Hall, Oxford*

CBI

Gower

Published by
Gower Publishing Company Limited
Gower House
Croft Road
Aldershot
Hants GU11 3HR

Marsh, Arthur
    Employee relations policy and decision making.
    1.   Industrial relations — Great Britain
    l.   Title
    331'.047'0941   HD8391

ISBN 0 566 00540 9

Printed in Great Britain by
Biddles Ltd, Guildford, Surrey

Contents

Appendices

Foreword

The CBI agreed with Arthur Marsh that there was a significant shortage of published information on the management of industrial relations. Much had been written about the operation and history of trade unions and there was then, as now, much debate on the external influences on industrial relations, such as employment legislation.

Two factors in particular led us to want this information gap filled. First, the improvement in competitiveness we so urgently need will require a greater stability and predictability in industrial relations than we have enjoyed in recent years. Secondly, the prime initiative in obtaining that improvement must come from within management. Managers will look for support from trade unions and government in that task but it is their decisions, their policy making and their professionalism which will count for most.

That was why we agreed to support this research by Arthur Marsh. We ourselves in the CBI need hard facts on which to base our policy decisions and our work generally on industrial relations. But I am certain that this book will be of much wider interest to observers of British industrial relations in general, in particular to individual companies as a comprehensive source of information on current practice.

T. Beckett
May 1982

1 Introduction

The Background

More changes have taken place in the British employee relations system
in the last decade than in the whole of the half century which preceded
the passing into law of the Industrial Relations Act 1971. The second
world war which ended in 1945 was characterised by unprecedented
co-operation between government, capital and labour. This served for
some years to confirm belief in the essential excellence of a system
handling labour relations which had been constructed, often with pain
and always with difficulty, in the previous century and extended by the
Whitley Committee recommendations at the end of the Kaiser's war.
Our methods of negotiation, of resolving conflict and of handling
relationships between employers and employed were, for a time,
universally accepted to be well-founded, stable and secure - indeed, as
it was frequently asserted, 'the best in the world'.

As the 1950s wore on, such remarks came to be regarded with less
certainty. For some years circumstances rather than system appeared to
be at fault. In a period in which the 'cold war' was uppermost in men's
minds it seems obvious to many that growing disorder in our workshops
and corresponding weaknesses in the authority of employers and
trade unions in resolving the situation were simply the result of the
machinations of 'politically motivated men' intent on disturbing the
balance of society. Shop stewards and their activities became subject
of much suspicious attention.

As the situation came better into focus it became clear that we were dealing less with subversion than with a sea change in the conduct of industrial relationships. During the 1960s, critical emphasis began to turn to the employee relations system itself. The National Board for Prices and Incomes, established in 1965, turned a merciless eye on pay practices. The legal basis of the system, established and more or less unchanged for three-quarters of a century, came increasingly into question. Were our traditional 'voluntary' methods so remarkable after all? Might they not be out of date and no longer in the public interest? The Donovan Commission on Trade Unions and Employers' Associations was set up to inquire and report. This it did in 1968. It was unfortunate for the Commission that it failed either to convert the trade unions to a modified form of traditional voluntarism or to persuade those who had become convinced that a more positive role for the law was now necessary to secure economic stability and industrial peace. The result was, in the short term, the defeat of the Wilson government at the hands of the Trades Union Congress in 1970 and the Industrial Relations Act 1971 by which the Heath administration which followed sought to place the system on a new, and in British terms, revolutionary, legalistic basis. By 1974 the Act had clearly failed in its main purpose but the system, for all the desire of some to put the clock back in the Trade Union and Labour Relations Act of that year, could, as was evident on all sides, never be the same again.

In the first place, the *positive* attractions for the law, once so slight in the trade union mind, assumed a new perspective as a result of the 1971 Act. If new rights could be created by Tories, why not by Socialists? While TULRA sought to restore the *status quo*, the Employment Protection Act 1975 aimed to raise the floor of rights both for individuals and for trade unions themselves, a package to be followed by a new initiative towards the achievement of industrial democracy. While the latter proved abortive, the development of codes of practice, begun under Conservatives, continued under Labour, leaving employers under closer and closer constraint in a situation which already provided rules on contracts of employment, on redundancy, on unfair dismissal, to which had been added tighter regulation on health and safety, on maternity leave and payment and on many other aspects of management-employee relations.

Second, two major changes of emphasis had become evident. For the first time in the late 1960s it had become plain that, if workplace relations in British companies seemed inadequate in any particular instance, it would be insufficient in future to attribute this to employees *alone*. Managements themselves would henceforward be held to have responsibility for *their* failings in organising and motivating their labour force. The emphasis shifted from an attitude in which

2

minimum attention to labour matters was all that was asked of employers to one in which they were expected on pay, procedures and attention to employee relations detail, to put their own houses in order. To this was added, from a number of sources in the 1970s, but particularly arising out of the draft Fifth Directive of the European Commission in 1974 and the Bullock Report of 1977, that effort was required from managements to improve the state of communication with, and participation by, employees in the management of companies.

Events since the fall of the Callaghan government in 1979 did little to change these essential emphases in British employee relations. Alterations or repeals involving the closed shop, trade union recognition, picketing, secondary boycott and recognised terms and conditions contained in the Employment Act 1980 did not sought to remove the pressures on employers to conduct their employee relations with greater expertise, wither greater system, and with greater success.

In one sense, therefore, the present survey, carried out at a point in time at the beginning of 1980, is a report on the state of play which had resulted from a decade of turmoil, pressure and achievement in British employee relations. It is an attempt to summarise what employees in manufacturing have done to adjust to a situation in which the old signposts became increasingly unclear and in which pressures for change became imperative as never before. Its immediate objects were more limited, as will be seen below.

Objects of the survey

The terms of reference on which the survey was conducted fell into two related parts - to investigate the extent of 'formalisation' of employee relations which might have been expected to result from the changes in law and practice which have characterised the past decade or more, and to inquire into the ways in which British boards of directors now approach the making of decisions and the establishment of policy in this area of management. Each part predicates the other. 'Formalisation' includes such matters as rule-making on terms and conditions of work, as the establishment and maintenance of procedures and routines for handling labour matters and as the encouragement of more structured approaches to pay, grievance, and dispute handling and other questions. These inevitably involve decisions and policy making whether implicit or explicit; they also involve the elevation of employee relations into a continuous process rather than a casual art and recognition of the fact that special expertise in employee relations is a necessary attribute of all managers, but especially of some, the employee relations specialist, under whatever title – 'personnel', 'labour', 'manpower', or whether 'director', 'controller', 'manager' or 'adviser'.

The report deals systematically with the information collected in an order which seems to be most natural in the circumstances. Having examined the general characteristics of the companies involved, it continues with a description of what now appears to be practice in the staffing of employee relations in companies of different types and sizes, moves on to the activities of boards of directors in the area of employee relations and then attempts to outline what the survey has to say about how employee relations are now, in day-to-day practice, being conducted, ending with a discussion of what policy and decision making processes appear to be involved.

There is no intention in the report to suggest that there is 'one best way' of conducting employee relations. Much depends on the circumstances of each company and on its preferred style of approach. But the survey did attempt, however imperfectly, to distinguish 'trends' and the reasons, where possible, for the emergence of such trends. Companies may prefer to follow, or to go their own way. The penalties for non-conformity may be slight and the rewards for successful innovation considerable. Underlying the report is the belief that, in either event, there is always something to be learned from what other folk are up to. At the very least it may concentrate the mind; at best, all tips may be of some use.

It goes without saying that the concepts and even the individual words used in a study of this kind may be familiar to some, difficult for others and even anathema to a few. Each chapter is prefaced by a brief account of the issues which appear to the writer to be paramount in the topic under discussion. This may be open to dispute as one man's view of the situation and this the writer wholly accepts. It may, nevertheless, be helpful to the reader to understand the general point of view from which the information given in the text has been approached and from which change in style and methods of handling employee relations have been measured.

Many years ago, at a time when the weaknesses of the Industrial Relations Act had already become apparent, but when its future and that of employee relations generally appeared to be even more uncertain than at present, I wrote that British industrial relations appeared to be dominated by three traditions, traditions so strong that they might deserve consideration as 'cults'. First there was the tradition of *privacy*, a preference for regarding practice as personal to situations, to companies and to unions, not to be opened to public scrutiny or evaluation. Second there was the tradition of *negotiation*, the notion that anything and everything can be made the subject of bargaining, a tradition beloved of trade unions and hardly resisted by managements. Thirdly, there was the tradition of *unstructure,* the belief that everything possible ought to be done by 'custom and practice', by word of mouth, by 'gentleman's agreement', the belief that institutions ought to be as loose as possible to allow for 'flexibility', for adaptation to circumstances. I suggested at that time that these traditions could only be maintained at some hazard to industry and the body politic. The reader may like, in addressing each subject below, to assess the extent to which these traditions have now been breached, for this is what I have done myself.

Survey methods

Our survey methods were dictated in part by resources available, in part by our intention to survey *company* practice at different levels and in part by our own experience. Previous surveys have been based on *establishments.*[1] This has clear advantages for some purposes. There are known distributions of such units of production by employees and by industry which can be used for sampling. Establishments are an unrivalled source of information about workplace relations, the study of which has been much to the fore in the past twenty years. But they tell us very little about companies themselves unless establishment and company are identical (i.e. unless a single establishment company is involved). Our own experience of attempting to use establishments as a basis for the study of company practice in multi-establishment concerns, is that establishment information about higher levels of management is inclined to be partial and often unreliable where employee relations are concerned. Though it is possible from establishment data to derive second and third levels of organisational information which can then be separately investigated[2] such an approach has its own difficulties and would have been beyond our resources.

It was, in any case, an approach which appeared unnatural given the variety of company type which the CBI information had to offer. This readily presented itself in terms of establishments which were companies in their own right and those which were subsidiaries of multi-establishment companies, of multi-establishment headquarter companies and of their divisions. This was ideal for our purposes, but carried with it the disadvantage that neither the CBI nor any other organisation has any data which would enable us to compare the

1 e.g. our own *Workplace Industrial Relations in Engineering* and the Warwick survey carried out in the winter of 1977-78; (see Brown, 1981).
2 e.g. in the Department of Employment survey carried out in connection with the Bullock Committee; (see Ian B. Knight, 1979).

distribution of our respondents with any known population drawn up on a like or similar basis. Our information represents a broad cross section of manufacturing industry rather than a statistical sample.

In practice we think that this is no great disadvantage. Any sample of companies is in the last resort drawn from those which are willing to respond. Even more important, it seems highly doubtful whether those factors which most easily present themselves as a sampling base, e.g. financial turnover, numbers employed, industry and location, have relevance to more than a limited number of employee relations practices. The bulk of the data with which we are dealing is, we believe, non-parametric by nature. We make no apology, therefore, for presenting this survey as based upon a representative group of companies operating in Britain rather than a statistical sample.

Our inquiry was conducted as follows. Initially we requested the Confederation of British Industry to derive from its membership records a random sample of member firms to a total size of about 3,000, excluding public corporations, i.e. of firms in the private sector of manufacturing industry. To these 3,000 companies we addressed an initial one page questionnaire (see Appendix 1, p.235) with two objects in mind. We wished first to establish what kind of company they were from the point of view of our survey; secondly, for companies which were willing to participate further, we gave notice that they would receive a second and much longer questionnaire and asked them to give us the name and telephone number of the director, executive or manager with whom we should thereafter communicate. In all we received about 1,200 replies to this initial questionnaire which established for us whether the company concerned was a single establishment company, whether it was an establishment or division (or group, or company or whatever title is used) of a multi-establishment company, or whether it was the headquarters of such a company. We also asked whether the respondent was British or foreign owned or controlled and whether, if it was a headquarters, it was a financial holding company only, with no employee relations function. About 180 companies replied to this effect, giving us a total of about 1,000 respondents, out of which some 350 ultimately completed our second questionnaire, 341 by the closing date of 31.5.1980. The situation is shown in Table 1 opposite.

The questionnaires used in the survey were drawn up after considerable consultation with companies large and small. We have to thank the Association of Independent Businesses for enabling us to discuss the single establishment company questionnaire with a number of their members and directors and senior executives of major multi-establishment companies, and particularly Mr Douglas Brooks, formerly of Hoover Ltd., for their advice on the even more complex questions addressed to companies of this type. The original research scheme provided that, in addition to a postal questionnaire we should interview 50 companies with a view to deepening our knowledge of their employee relations practices, particularly in the area of collective bargaining and the staffing of employee relations. A list of these companies is to be found in Appendix 2, p.237. To the directors and managers of these companies who gave us so freely of their time and insights we are greatly indebted and also to those who completed so patiently and accurately our long (and no doubt tiresome) questionnaires.

The form of this inquiry, its emphasis and content, and its specific objectives, were agreed in consultation with Richard Worsley, now Director, Social Affairs Directorate, Confederation of British Industry, and at that time its Deputy Director (Policy). Day-to-day problems were adjusted and resolved with his assistant, Ewen Peters, now of the Scottish Development Authority. We thank them both for their courtesy, kindness and co-operation in smoothing the path so admirably for the work which we have done. Needless to say, they have no responsibility for the opinions we have expressed; these, warts and all, are entirely our own. Jenni Atkinson, for her patient attention to detail in supervising the circulation and processing of the questionnaires, Anthony Hardie, for his skill and assistance in seeing the data through the computer and Olive Woods for her clerical help, have all played a part in making this study possible.

Table 1
Number of respondents and rates of response

	Initial questionnaire	Second questionnaire	Per cent completed
Holding cos.	178	-	0.0
Single est. cos.	486	156	32.1
Ests. multi.	125	54	43.2
Divisions multi.	96	29	30.2
HQ multi.	316	102	32.3
Total	1,201	341	28.4

In the tabulations which follow each chapter and to which reference is made in parentheses in the text, *establishments,* whether they are single establishment companies or establishments of multis are indicated by a chapter number, followed by a decimal point (.) and a plain ordinal number (e.g. *Membership of Employers' Associations* is Table 2.6, being the sixth table in Chapter 2); multi establishment companies and divisions of multi establishment companies are distinguished by a zero (0) after the decimal point (e.g. the corresponding Table on *Membership of Employers' Associations* is 2.06). Each chapter is followed by a reference list of books and articles relevant to it and by the relevant tabulations.

2 The survey companies

Size and organisation

The 156 single establishment companies included in the survey employed some 29,000 employees and the 54 establishments of multi-establishment companies almost 23,000 (2.2). (Single establishment companies tend, as has been noted elsewhere, to be smaller than establishments of multis[1]. On average, the former employed 188 people and the latter 420.) Nine hundred and thirty-eight thousand were employed by the 102 multi-establishment companies and 39,400 by the 29 divisions of multis (2.03). The whole survey thus covered a total labour force of 1.03 millions.

The companies were distributed widely over the manufacturing sector of the economy. Forty-two per cent of them fell into engineering and shipbuilding for the purposes of the official Standard Industrial Classification, 9.4 per cent into textiles and clothing, with smaller percentages in all manufacturing groups. A few companies, no doubt because of their connections with manufacturing, turned out to be primarily related to distribution and services (2.5, 2.05). Because of the mix of multi-establishment and single establishment companies and divisions, it is, as already noted, not possible to compare the distribution as a whole with any nationally available data, since this relates to establishments only. It seems likely, however, that engineering is over-represented and to some degree chemicals also, textiles, bricks, pottery and timber being somewhat under-represented.

1 Brown W. (1981), Table 3.1.

Not all the *single establishment companies* in the survey were small in terms of numbers employed. While their median size was about 75, and while 50 of them employed fewer than 50 people (and one of these as few as 6), 14 employed more than 500, the average company in this size group finding work for more than 900 and the largest for 2,150. Some *multi-establishment companies* did not attain this size. While each company on average employed more than 900, 52 per cent only employed more than 1,000 manual workers (2.2, 2.3, 2.4; 2.04 a and b). Some were therefore small compared with the largest single establishment companies. The criterion laid down for the inclusion of such a company (see Appendix 1, p.235) was simply that it should be an 'organisation with subsidiary groups, businesses, or establishments'. Many companies commonly regarded as 'small' fulfil such a criterion in that they have branch factories or depots, many of them separately registered under the Companies Acts. It should be borne in mind, therefore, when examining the results of the survey, that in referring, for example, to the'headquarters of a multi-establishment company', this does not in all cases imply that the head office of a giant combine is involved. Nevertheless, *most* multi-establishment companies in the survey were large in this sense; many of them were, indeed, household names.

We have been unable in this survey to do justice to the organisational complexity of many of our respondents, especially the larger ones. Some were unable, in the small compass provided, to tell us in detail precisely how they were set up for employee relations purposes. Something of the difficulty of the situation can be appreciated from the fact that, taking the survey as a whole, we found ourselves attempting to describe arrangements at a total of 102 multi-establihsments, 711 subsidiary companies or divisions and no fewer than 3,202 establishments, all of which no doubt varied to a greater or lesser extent in their handling of employee relations. Our treatment is inevitably broad brush in many respects.

The survey nevertheless throws some light on multi-establishment company organisation in general. It will already have been noted by the reader that of the original 494 headquarters of multis replying to our original questionnaire 178 (or 36 per cent) claimed to have no employee relations functions at that level. All but 14 of the 102 headquarters which replied to our second questionnaire, and which therefore had an employee relations function, had also some kind of divisional arrangement for management purposes. Between 2 and 8 divisions was the modal number, though many had more. Most companies had between 2 and 8 establishments, but 4 had one only and 5 had over 100 (2.01).

Rather more than one in five of all the companies in the survey reported that they were foreign owned or controlled. The extent of such control varied according to the four main survey groups as Table 2 shows.

Table 2

Companies reporting foreign ownership or control

| | Numbers of companies reporting foreign ownership or control | | | |
| | First questionnaire | | Second questionnaire | |
	Number	Per cent of respondents	Number	Per cent of respondents
Single establishment companies	20	4.1	3	1.9
Establishments of multis	77	61.6	32	59.3
Divisions of multis	68	70.8	16	55.2
Multi-establishment companies	68	21.5	22	21.6
All respondents	233	22.8	73	21.4

Four per cent only of the single establishment respondents to our first questionnaire reported that they were foreign owned or controlled. Many were, of course, family concerns and unlikely to have non-British connections of this kind. Self-evidently, perhaps, it is more likely that multi-establishment company situations are involved in foreign ownership, as they were in 213 instances in our first questionnaire responses and 70 in our second. Of the headquarters of such companies replying to both questionnaires rather more than 21 per cent reported foreign ownership or control; the incidence was much more frequent among *establishments* (about 60 per cent) and, in the first questionnaire, among *divisions* (71 per cent). No explanation for this readily suggests itself and the divisional proportion fell in response to the second questionnaire.

Employers' association membership

Seventy-four per cent of the establishments covered by the Warwick survey of 1977-78 said that they were directly or indirectly in membership of the Confederation of British Industry, 29 per cent of establishments directly so;[1] 75 per cent also replied that they were in membership of an employers' organisation. Very likely some of these were not 'employers' associations' for employee relations purposes, as the Warwick study admits. Our own figures were more reliable in this respect but biased, of course, by initial CBI membership. Fifty-seven per cent of all individual establishments were members of one or more associations and 69 per cent of multi-establishment companies and divisions at one level or another. Among the latter, membership of up to six associations was not unknown. Almost 7 out of 10 of the establishments and almost 8 out of 10 headquarters and divisions who were members claimed that they were active in the sense of attending meetings and serving on committees and encouraging their subsidiaries to do so (2.6, 2.06). On this finding, associations are very much alive where CBI members are concerned. There is evidence elsewhere in the survey that information and advice of associations continues to be widely sought on employee relations matters generally, but especially on pay settlements (Chapter 8). Larger companies in multi-association membership also attempt, at least from time to time to coordinate relationships between them.

Trade unionism

Four out of 10 single establishment companies and 3 out of 10 establishments of multis in the survey recognised no manual trade unions, 8 out of 10 of the former and almost half the latter recognised no non-manual unions. Divisions of multis were 17 per cent non-unionised for manual workers and 40 per cent for non-manuals. The extent of multi-unionism was, as other sources have also shown, less than is often believed. On the average, organised establishments had two manual unions and between one and two non-manual; divisions had three manual and two non-manual, while multi-establishment companies reported an average of five and between two and three respectively. A few, however, had more than nine (2.7a and b, 2.07a and b).

Compared with a decade ago the survey showed a modest but significant shift of opinion among companies in favour of trade unionism, particularly for non-manual employees, and, especially in the case of multi-establishment companies, a slight change in favour of

1 Brown, W. (1981), Table 2.6.

12

organisation of managers also. The closed shop was however over-whelmingly unacceptable among all respondents, though marginally less so than it was said to have been ten years earlier (2.8 and 2.08). Pressure or claims for trade union recognition were reported by divisions and multi-establishment companies as having been more widespread than by establishments. On the average, it seems, each multi and division had had between one and two claims over that period, individual establishments less than one and single establishment companies less than one-half. Thirteen per cent of a total of 336 recorded claims had involved the procedure laid down in the Employment Protection Act ss.11-16 now repealed (1.9 and 1.09).

Industrial action

In the context of the troubled 1960s and 70s, 1979 was not the year in which the largest number of officially recorded stoppages began. It was, however, a year in which an exceptionally large number of stoppages were in progress and an exceptionally large number of workers were involved. Moreover it witnessed the highest number of working days lost in any year in the present century except for the years 1912, 1919, 1920 and 1921 and the general strike of 1926. It also had the greatest number of 'large' stoppages as a proportion of all stoppages in the past two decades. One such stoppage lasting for 11 weeks was in the public sector and falls outside the scope of this survey; two others fall within it. These were the national road haulage strike which went on for 6 weeks from 2 January 1979 and the escalating one and two day stoppages which occurred in the engineering industry in all parts of the UK between 6 August and 4 November. Both strikes gave rise to an unusually high level of picketing. On this ground alone the data collected as a result of the survey is not only unusual, but unique, since no other statistical information about the practice has ever before been compiled.[1]

Of the 131 multi establishment companies and divisions, 31 reported that they had no information about industrial action in their establishments. Some noted that it was not their practice to collect such information, others that it existed in their subsidiaries or establishments but was not centrally filed. Of the 100 companies remaining, 18 per cent claimed that they had no industrial action of any kind during 1979; 71 per cent had had withdrawals of labour, almost as many overtime bans with a lesser incidence of go-slows and blacking (2.010, 2.011 and 2.012). This seems hardly surprising in the

1 Tables 2.13-15 on picketing have already been published in *Personnel Management Review* and are reprinted here with the permission of the editor.

circumstances and no doubt represented less action on an established basis. The companies and divisions were large, action being spread over almost 800,000 employees. Almost 60 per cent said that they had experienced picketing.

It is of course, from the establishment level that the most comprehensive and accurate industrial action information is likely to be derived. At this level, 130 of the 210 establishments in the survey (or almost 62 per cent) reported no industrial action of any kind in 1979. This was not unexpected. In 1967-68 when short domestic stoppages were probably more frequent than they are now, almost 40 per cent of 432 engineering establishments reported no such actions; more recently the Warwick survey taken in the winter of 1977-78, which, like the present survey, covered manufacturing establishments of all kinds, reported 'no industrial action' at 54.3 per cent of the 970 establishments concerned (Brown 1981). Some part of any difference between this and the Warwick survey may be accounted for by the 'size effect'. Both surveys confirm that smaller establishments are less action prone than larger ones; the Warwick survey excluded establishments employing 50 or less, which made up 29 per cent of the present sample (2.11, 2.12). Almost one-quarter of our 210 establishments had experienced picketing in 1979.

The picketing experience of the 51 affected establishments was complex. Of the 42 which had experienced stoppages of work, only 16 had experienced picketing in relation to them, and that of these only 2 had arisen as a result of strikes which originated *within the establishments themselves* in an 'internal dispute'. The remainder had arisen either out of national stoppages in the industry of the employer himself (particularly out of engineering), or out of 'unrelated disputes', especially the national road haulage strike. Alternatively, but to a much smaller extent, they had arisen out of disputes involving suppliers and customers. The order of importance of various sources of picketing in 1979 is shown in Tables 2.14 and 2.15. Fewer than 1 per cent of the 210 establishments had, therefore, been picketed as a result of a dispute arising in their own works; almost 7 per cent had been affected by picketing arising from their own workers acting in support of a national stoppage in their own industry; almost twice that percentage had been affected by 'unrelated disputes' and a little over 7 per cent by actions at suppliers and customers. Given that 90 picketing occasions were spread over 51 establishments, 'multiple sources' were not uncommon. In all, there were 7, all relating to a combination between 'unrelated', 'supplier' and 'customer' picketing. The situation became even more complex where multi-establishment companies were concerned (2.013).

In such circumstances it might be expected that at the majority of

14

establishments picketing was conducted by employees other than their own. This was indeed the case (2.16, the figures in brackets resulting from an additional inquiry made to those who had not replied to the question). Of the 16 establishments with 'own' and national 'own industry' disputes, 13 were picketed by 'own' employees and 3 by 'strangers'. In the remaining 35 establishments only 3 were picketed by 'own' employees. This 35 was composed chiefly of 'unrelated disputes'. We were not able to determine where *both* 'own' pickets and 'strangers' were jointly involved and our information remains no more than approximate.

'Secondary' picketing to the extent of that carried on in 1979-80 had occurred relatively rarely in British industrial history, at most at intervals of 20 years, and is invariably associated with some national or community based dispute. When it happens 'flying' pickets, 'mass' picketing and some degree of civil disorder results. This survey suggests that, even in such extreme circumstances, fewer manufacturing establishments are affected than may have been popularly supposed. It also suggests that in more 'normal' years in which some internal stoppages in companies may be accompanied by picketing, that number may be supposed to be very small; the resultant picketing is also likely to be predominantly peaceful in character. This probably explains why the concept of the lawfulness of 'peaceful picketing' which became accepted about a century ago, has tended to be seriously challenged in parliament and elsewhere only in the extreme circumstances of the kind experienced in 1979-80.

Unfair dismissal

The experience of the 341 companies in the survey in respect of unfair dismissal is given in tables 2.17 and 2.014. During the previous five years 42 per cent of single establishment companies had had claims and 61 per cent of establishments of multis. On the average of all 210 such companies, each had had one claim during that period; those subject to claims had had two on average, but no fewer than 30 companies had had more than two claims; three had had six or seven. Multi-establishment companies and divisions had, understandably, been even more involved, only 17 per cent having had *no* claims at all, the average number for all companies being respectively 12 and 3. It is perhaps a sign of the times that very few companies of any of the four descriptions expressed themselves as concerned about publicity in the press about such cases (4 per cent), or about the amount of the awards made (under 3 per cent). Some single establishment companies (21 per cent) apparently found the conciliation procedure tiresome, but the greatest difficulty recorded by all lay in the time taken in preparation and spent attending a tribunal.

References

Anderman, S.D. *The Law on Unfair Dismissal,* Butterworth, 1978.

Brown, W. (ed.) *The Changing Contours of British Industrial Relations,* Basil Blackwell, 1981.

Clifton, R. and Tatton-Browne, C. *Impact of Employment Legislation in Small Firms,* Department of Employment Research Paper No. 6, 1979.

Daniel, W.W. and Stilgoe, E. *The Impact of Employment Protection Laws,* Policy Studies Institute, 1978.

Department of Employment, 'Large Industrial Stoppages, 1960-79', *Employment Gazette,* September 1980, pp. 994-999.

Edwards, P.K. 'Plant Size and Strike-proneness', *Oxford Bulletin of Economics and Statistics,* Vol. 42, May 1980.

Edwards, P.K. 'The Strike-proneness of British Manufacturing Establishments', *British Journal of Industrial Relations,* Vol. XIX, No. 2, July 1981.

Grant, W. and Marsh, D. *The CBI,* Hodder and Stoughton, 1977.

Knight, I.B. *Company Organisation and Work Participation,* HMSO, 1979.

Knowles, K.G.J.C. *Strikes,* Basil Blackwell, 1954.

Marsh, A.I., Evans, E.O. and Garcia, P. *Workplace Industrial Relations in Engineering,* Kogan Page and EEF, November 1971.

Marsh, A.I. and Gillies, J.G. 'The Incidence of Picketing in 1979', *Personnel Management Review,* January 1979, pp.14-22.

Shorey, J. 'The Size of Work Unit and Strike Incidence', *Journal of Industrial Economics,* Vol. 23, March 1975.

Smith, C.T.B., Clifton, R., Makeham, P., Creigh, S.W. and Burn, R.V. *Strikes in Britain,* Department of Employment Manpower Paper No. 15, 1978.

Tabulations

The survey companies

2.1 Type of business

	Single establishment company		Individual establishment multi	
	Number	Per cent	Number	Per cent
Partnership	3	1.9	0	0.0
Private company	140	89.8 ⎫	48	88.9
Public company	12	7.7 ⎭		
Branch of parent company	-	-	6	11.0
No response	1	0.6	0	0.0
	156	100.0	54	100.0

2.2 Establishments by numbers of manual and non-manual employees

Numbers of employees	Single establishment			
	Number of establishments	Per cent total	Number of employees	Per cent total
50 or less	50	32.0	1,563	5.3
51–100	41	26.3	2,926	10.0
101–250	33	21.2	5,314	18.1
251–500	18	11.5	6,590	22.4
501 and over	14	9.0	12,985	44.2
	156	100.0	28,378	100.0

	Multi-establishment			
	Number of establishments	Per cent total	Number of employees	Per cent total
50 or less	12	22.2	373	1.6
51–100	6	11.1	416	1.8
101–250	13	24.1	2,325	10.2
251–500	5	9.3	2,222	9.8
501 and over	18	33.3	17,370	76.6
	54	100.0	22,706	100.0

2.3 Number of employees
Manual

	Single establishment company		Individual establishment multi	
	Number	Per cent	Number	Per cent
Under 25	27	17.3	9	16.7
25–50	40	25.7	6	11.1
51–100	37	23.8	9	16.7
101–250	30	19.2	9	16.7
251–500	15	9.6	9	16.7
501–1000	3	1.9	8	14.8
Over 1000	3	1.9	2	3.7
No response	1	0.6	2	3.7
	156	100.0	54	100.0

2.4 Number of employees
Non-manual

	Single establishment company		Individual establishment multi	
	Number	Per cent	Number	Per cent
Under 25	91	58.3	16	29.5
25–50	26	16.7	10	18.5
51–100	19	12.2	7	13.0
101–250	11	7.1	9	16.7
251–500	5	3.2	7	13.0
501–1000	0	0.0	4	7.4
Over 1000	1	0.6	1	1.9
No response	3	1.9	0	0.0
	156	100.0	54	100.0

2.5 Distribution by industry

	Single establishment company		Individual establishment multi	
	Number	Per cent	Number	Per cent
Food, drink, tobacco	10	6.4	1	1.9
Coal, petroleum products	1	0.6	-	-
Chemicals	10	6.4	6	11.0
Metal manufacture	6	3.8	3	5.5
Engineering, shipbuilding	72	46.3	29	53.7
Textiles, clothing	18	11.6	3	5.6
Bricks, pottery, timber	7	4.5	1	1.9
Paper and printing	11	7.1	2	3.7
Other manufacturing	10	6.4	7	12.9
Construction	3	1.9	-	-
Transport	1	0.6	-	-
Distribution	3	1.9	-	-
Services	1	0.6	1	1.9
No response	3	1.9	1	1.9
	156	100.0	54	100.0

2.6 Membership of employers' associations (excl CBI)

Companies	Single establishment company		Individual establishment multi	
	Number	Per cent	Number	Per cent
Member of:				
No employers' association	66	42.3	25	46.3
1 association	76	48.7	21	36.9
2 associations	10	6.5	7	13.0
3 associations	3	1.9	1	1.9
4 associations	1	0.6	-	-
	156	100.0	54	100.0
of which: active in associations	57	37.8	24	46.3

2.7 Number of trade unions recognised
a. Manual workers

	Single establishment company		Individual establishment multi	
	Number	Per cent	Number	Per cent
No union	63	40.4	15	27.8
1 union	61	39.2	20	37.0
2 unions	16	10.3	10	18.5
3 unions	8	5.1	4	7.4
4 unions	6	3.8	2	3.7
5 unions	1	0.6	1	1.9
6 unions	1	0.6	2	3.7
7 unions	-	-		
	156	100.0	54	100.0

Average number of unions per establishment:
all respondents	1.0	1.4
with TUs	1.6	2.0

2.7 Number of trade unions recognised
b. Non-manual workers

| | Single establishment company | | Individual establishment multi | |
	Number	Per cent	Number	Per cent
No union	125	80.2	25	46.3
1 union	23	14.7	19	35.2
2 unions	5	3.2	6	11.1
3 unions	2	1.3	3	5.6
4 unions	1	0.6	1	1.9
5 unions	-	-	-	-
6 unions	-	-	-	-
7 unions	-	-	-	-
	156	100.0	54	100.0

Average number of unions per establishment:		
all respondents	0.3	0.8
with TUs	1.4	1.5

2.8 Attitudes of companies to trade unionism

| | Single establishment company | | Individual establishment multi | |
| | Today | In the past * | Today | In the past * |
	Per cent		Per cent	
In favour of trade unionism	50.6	44.9	59.3	50.0
In favour of organisation of staff employees	20.5	15.4	29.6	20.4
In favour of organisation of managers	4.5	6.4	1.9	1.9
Opposed to post-entry closed shop	78.8	80.8	75.9	81.5

* Ten or more years ago.

2.9 Pressures and claims for trade union recognition in the past five years

	Single establishment		Individual establishment			
	Number	Per cent	Number		Per cent	
	Cos. cases	Cos. cases	Cos. cases		Cos. cases	
Companies subject to pressures or claims	44 64	28.2	24	46	44.4	
of which: one only	30 30	68.3 46.9	16	16	66.7 34.8	
two	10 20	22.7 31.2	3	6	12.5 13.0	
three	2 6	4.5 9.4	2	6	8.3 13.0	
more than three	2 8	4.5 12.5	3	18	12.5 39.2	
	44 64	100.0 100.0	24	46	100.0 100.0	
Claims involving s. 11 EP Act	12	17.7	5		9.3	
of which: one only	11 11	91.7 84.6	2	2	25.0 33.3	
two	1 2	8.3 15.4	3	6	75.0 66.7	
	12 13	100.0 100.0	5	8	100.0 100.0	

2.10 Industrial actions in 1979

Industrial action	Single establishment company		Individual establishment multi	
	Percentages of		Percentages of	
	companies affected	companies not affected	companies affected	companies not affected
Withdrawals of labour:	17.9 (40)	82.1	25.9 (17)	74.1
Overtime bans	9.6 (29)	90.4	18.5 (18)	81.5
Go-slows etc.	2.6 (5)	97.4	11.1 (9)	88.9
Blacking-out	1.9 (5)	98.1	0.0 (0)	100.0
Blacking-in	3.2 (9)	96.8	1.0 (1)	98.1
Picketing: own dispute	1.3 (2)	98.7	0.0 (0)	100.0
national dispute	7.0 (19)	93.0	5.6 (3)	94.6
at suppliers	1.9 (8)	98.1	9.3 (5)	90.7
at customers	1.9 (6)	98.1	3.8 (4)	96.2
'unrelated'	10.9 (27)	89.1	22.2 (16)	77.8
Own labour force picketing	5.8		7.4	
Not own labour force picketing	6.4		14.8	

( ) number of occasions.

2.11 Establishments with no experience of industrial action of any kind in 1979 by numbers employed (210 CBI establishments)

Number of employees	Establishments		Employees		All estab- lish- ments	Per cent with no industrial action
	Number	Per cent	Number	Per cent		
50 or less	52	40.0	1,604	6.7	62	83.9
51—100	31	23.8	2,152	9.1	47	66.0
101—250	25	19.3	4,489	18.9	46	54.3
251—500	12	9.2	4,245	17.8	23	52.2
501 and over	10	7.7	11,291	47.5	32	31.2
	130	100.0	23,781	100.0	210	61.9

2.12 Establishments with experience of industrial action and picketing of any kind in 1979, by numbers employed (210 CBI establishments)

Number of employees	Industrial action Establishments		Picketing Establishments		Employees		All Estab- lish- ments	Percent with picketing
	Number	Percent	Number	Percent	Number	Percent		
50 or less	10	16.1	10	19.6	334	2.0	62	16.1
51 — 100	16	34.0	12	23.5	938	6.7	47	25.5
101 — 250	21	45.6	12	23.5	1,835	12.4	46	26.1
251 — 500	11	47.8	3	5.9	1,125	7.6	23	13.0
501 and over	22	68.7	14	27.5	10,504	71.3	32	31.1
	80	38.1	51	100.0	14,736	100.0	210	24.3

2.13 Industrial action and picketing reported at 210 CBI establishments in 1979

	Establishments*		Occasions	
	Number	Per cent	Number	Per cent
Withdrawals of labour:	42	20.0	57	42.9
Overtime bans	25	11.9	47	35.4
Go-slows etc.	10	4.8	14	10.5
Blacking-in	6	2.9	10	7.5
Blacking-out	3	1.4	5	3.7
Any internal action	80	38.1	133	100.0
Picketing:				
own dispute	2	0.9	2	2.2
national dispute	14	6.7	22	24.5
involving suppliers	8	3.8	13	14.4
involving customers	5	2.4	10	11.1
'unrelated'	29	13.8	43	47.8
Any picketing	51	24.3	90	100.0

*Some establishments reported more than one industrial action or source of picketing.

2.14 Picketing and blacking reported at 210 CBI establishments in 1979.*

Establishments with	Establishments		Employees	
	Number	Per cent	Number	Per cent
No experience of industrial action of any kind	130	61.9	23,781	45.6
Internal stoppages of work, including those arising out of own industry disputes	42	20.0	19,380	37.2
of which picketing took place in	16	38.1	7,539	38.9
Picketing arising out of 'unrelated' disputes	29	13.8	5,939	11.4
Affected by picketing in connection with disputes:				
involving suppliers	8	3.8	2,750	5.3
involving customers	5	2.4	326	0.6
Affected by blacking of goods:				
in	6	2.8	2,517	4.8
out	3	1.4	828	1.6
All establishments	210	100.0	52,084	100.0

*CBI Survey: single establishment companies and establishments of multi establishment companies.

2.15 Source of dispute giving rise to picketing at 51 CBI establishments

Source of dispute	Establishments	
	Number	Per cent
'Unrelated'	24	47.0
National - own industry	14	27.5
'Unrelated' and supplier	4	7.9
Customer only	2	3.9
Own dispute only	2	3.9
Supplier only	2	3.9
'Unrelated' and customer	1	2.0
Supplier and customer	2	3.9
All sources	51	100.0

2.16 Sources of pickets at 51 picketed establishments

Source of pickets	Number	Per cent
Own employees	13 (16)	25.5
Not own employees	18 (35)	35.2
No response	20 (-)	39.3
All picketed establishments	51 (51)	100.0

2.17 Claims for unfair dismissal in the past five years

	Single establishment				Individual establishment			
	Number		Per cent		Number		Per cent	
	Cos.	Cases	Cos.	Cases	Cos.	Cases	Cos.	Cases
Companies subject to claims	65	137	41.7		33	67	61.1	
of which:								
one only	29	29	44.6	21.2	15	15	45.5	22.4
two	15	30	23.1	21.9	9	18	27.3	26.9
three	13	39	20.0	28.4	4	12	12.1	17.9
four	4	16	6.2	11.7	4	16	12.1	23.9
five	2	10	3.1	7.3	0	0	0.0	0.0
six	1	6	1.5	4.4	1	6	3.0	8.9
seven	1	7	1.5	5.1	0	0	0.0	0.0
	65	137	100.0	100.0	33	67	100.0	100.0
Average per establishment								
N = total			0.9				1.2	
N = subject to claims			2.1				2.0	
Companies noting sources of difficulty:*								
conciliation procedure	17		21.5		6		16.7	
preparation time	43		54.4		21		58.3	
amount of award	2		2.5		3		8.3	
press publicity	3		3.8		0		0.0	
other difficulty	14		17.8		6		16.7	
	79		100.0		36		100.0	

*Some companies gave more than one difficulty.

2.01 Multi-establishment companies: number of subsidiary companies, businesses or divisions and establishments

Size group	Multi-establishment companies		Divisions Establishments/ divisions	
	Number	Per cent	Number	Per cent
No divisions	14	13.7	-	-
One only	2	2.0	2	-
2—4	41	40.2	131	19.9
5—8	24	23.4	148	22.6
9—12	8	7.9	71	10.9
13—16	2	2.0	28	4.4
17—25	5	4.9	95	14.5
26—50	3	2.9	126	19.2
Over 50	1	1.0	56	8.5
No response or not known	2	2.0	-	-
	102	100.0	657	100.0

			Establishments	
One only	4	3.9	4	-
2—4	37	36.3	114	3.9
5—8	23	22.5	143	4.9
9—12	8	7.9	83	2.8
13—16	3	2.9	41	1.4
17—25	11	10.8	224	7.6
26—50	7	6.9	293	10.0
51—100	1	1.0	58	2.0
Over 100	5	4.9	1978	67.4
No response or not known	3	2.9	-	-
	102	100.0	2938	100.0

2.02 Divisions of multis: number of establishments

Size group	Divisions of multis		Establishments	
	Number	Per cent	Number	Per cent
One only	10	34.5	10	9.2
2–4	8	27.6	20	18.5
5–8	4	13.8	26	24.1
9–12	3	10.3	33	30.6
Over 13	1	3.4	19	17.6
No response	3	10.3	–	–
	29	100.0	108	100.0

2.03 Companies and divisions: total manual and staff employees

Numbers of employees	Multi-establishment companies			
	Number of companies	Per cent total	Number of employees	Per cent total
50 or less	1	1.0	38	negligible
51–100	7	6.9	611	negligible
101–250	7	6.9	953	0.1
251–500	13	12.7	4,540	0.5
501 and over	72	70.6	932,204	99.4
No response	2	1.9	–	–
	102	100.0	938,346	100.0

	Divisions of multis			
	Number of divisions	Per cent total	Number of employees	Per cent total
50 or less	1	3.4	31	0.1
51–100	6	20.7	391	1.0
101–250	3	10.3	389	1.0
251–500	2	6.9	705	1.8
501 and over	17	58.7	37,901	96.1
	29	100.0	39,417	100.0

2.04a Number of employees: manual

	Multi-establishment company		Division of multi	
	Number	Per cent	Number	Per cent
Under 25	1	1.0	1	3.4
26—50	4	4.0	5	17.3
51—100	8	7.8	4	13.8
101—250	11	10.8	5	17.3
251—500	8	7.8	1	3.4
501—1000	15	14.7	6	20.7
Over 1000	53	52.0	7	24.1
No response	2	1.7	0	0.0
	102	100.0	29	100.0

2.04b Number of employees: non-manual

	Multi-establishment company		Division of multi	
	Number	Per cent	Number	Per cent
Under 25	5	4.9	4	13.8
26—50	10	9.8	5	17.3
51—100	9	8.8	1	3.4
101—250	11	10.8	3	10.3
251—500	14	13.7	6	20.7
501—1000	7	6.9	7	24.2
Over 1000	43	42.2	3	10.3
No response	3	2.9	0	0.0
	102	100.0	29	100.0

2.05 Distribution by industry

	Multi-establishment companies		Divisions of multis	
	Number	Per cent	Number	Per cent
Food, drink, tobacco	15	14.7	2	6.9
Coal, petroleum prod.	5	4.9	1	3.4
Chemicals	8	7.8	3	10.4
Metal manufacture	2	3.0	2	6.9
Engineering, shipbuilding	33	32.3	11	37.9
Textiles, clothing	10	9.8	1	3.4
Bricks, pottery, timber	5	4.9	2	6.9
Paper and printing	7	6.9	3	10.4
Other manufacturing	6	5.9	3	10.4
Construction	4	3.9	1	3.4
Transport	1	1.0	0	0.0
Distribution	1	1.0	0	0.0
Services	5	4.9	0	0.0
No response	0	0.0	0	0.0
	102	100.0	29	100.0

2.06 Membership of employers' associations

	Multi-establishment companies		Divisions of multis	
	Number	Per cent	Number	Per cent
In membership of employers' associations on:				
No establishment	29	28.4	12	41.4
A minority of establishments	19	18.9	1	3.4
A majority of establishments	32	31.4	1	3.4
All establishments	22	21.6	15	51.7
All with membership	73	71.6	17	58.5
Of which:				
active in associations	57	78.1	12	70.6
encourage lower levels to be active in assn's	57	78.1	11	64.7
	73	100.0	17	100.0
Of which in membership of:				
1 association	35	48.0	16	94.1
2 associations	14	19.2	1	5.9
3 associations	15	20.5	-	-
4 associations	5	6.8	-	-
5 associations	0	0.0	-	-
6 associations	3	4.1	-	-
more than 6 associations	1	1.4	-	-
Of which attempt to co-ordinate relations with different assn's:				
generally	13	17.8	1	5.9
in some cases	33	45.2	2	11.8

2.07a Number of trade unions recognised: manual workers

	Multi-establishment company		Division of multis	
	Number	Per cent	Number	Per cent
No union	12	11.8	5	17.2
1 union	20	19.6	10	34.5
2 unions	11	10.8	3	10.4
3 unions	9	8.8	4	13.8
4 unions	9	8.8	2	6.9
5 unions	11	10.8	3	10.4
6 unions	3	2.9	1	3.4
7 unions	10	9.8	1	3.4
8 unions	6	5.9	0	–
9 unions or more	11	10.8	0	
	102	100.0	29	100.0
Average number of unions per company or division:				
all respondents	4.3		2.2	
with TUs	4.9		2.7	

2.07b Number of trade unions recognised: non-manual workers

	Multi-establishment company		Division of multi	
	Number	Per cent	Number	Per cent
No union	32	31.4	12	41.4
1 union	21	20.6	8	27.6
2 unions	15	14.7	4	13.8
3 unions	11	10.8	2	6.9
4 unions	6	5.9	3	10.3
5 unions	6	5.9	-	-
6 unions	6	5.9	-	-
7 unions	3	2.8	-	-
9 or more	2	2.0	-	-
	102	100.0	29	100.0

Average number of
unions per company
or division:

all respondents	2.1		1.2
with TUs	2.4		2.0

2.08 Attitudes of companies to trade unionism

	Multi-establishment company		Division of multi	
	Today	In the * past	Today	In the* past
	Per cent		Per cent	
In favour of trade unionism	69.6	61.8	65.5	55.2
In favour of organisation of staff employees	52.0	24.5	44.8	17.2
In favour of organisation of managers	11.8	5.7	3.4	0.0
Opposed to post-entry closed shop	64.7	70.6	75.9	82.8

* Ten or more years ago.

2.09 Pressures and claims for trade union recognition in the past five years

	Multi-establishment co.				Division of multi			
	Number		Per cent		Number		Per cent	
	Cos.	Cases	Cos.	Cases	Cos.	Cases	Cos.	Cases
Companies subject to pressures or claims	60	155	58.8	-	20	71	69.0	-
of which:								
1 only	18	18	30.0	11.6	7	7	35.0	9.8
2	16	32	26.7	20.6	2	4	10.0	5.6
3	14	42	23.3	27.2	3	9	15.0	12.8
more than 3	12	63	16.7	40.6	8	51	40.0	71.8
	60	155	100.0	100.0	20	71	100.0	100.0
Claims involving s. 11 EP Act	13	19	12.7	-	7	6	24.1	-
of which:								
1 only	9	9	67.2	47.4	6	6	85.7	100.0
2	2	4	15.4	21.0	-	-	-	-
3	2	6	15.4	31.6	1	-	14.3	-
	13	19	100.0	100.0	7	6	100.0	100.0

2.010 Industrial actions in 1979

	Multi-establishment companies Percentages of companies		Divisions of multis Percentages of divisions	
	Affected	Not affected	Affected	Not affected
All companies and* divisions	80.8	19.2	86.4	13.6
Withdrawals of labour	66.6 (808)	33.4	45.4 (16)	54.6
Overtime bans	61.5 (109)	38.5	59.0 (16)	41.0
Go-slows etc.	39.7 (57)	60.3	31.8 (10)	68.2
Blacking-out	10.2 (14)	89.8	4.5 (1)	95.5
Blacking-in	9.0 (21)	91.0	0.0 (0)	100.0
Picketing:				
own establishments own employees	25.6 (33)	74.4	22.7 (7)	77.3
sympathetic action, own establishment in favour of a second establishment	8.9 (8)	91.1	0.0 (0)	100.0
national dispute	14.1 (16)	85.9	27.2 (6)	72.8
dispute involving suppliers	8.9 (11)	91.1	4.5 (7)	95.5
dispute involving customers	2.6 (2)	97.4	0.0 (0)	100.0
'unrelated' dispute	37.1 (32)	62.9	22.7 (5)	77.3

* All percentages relate to 78 multi-establishment companies and 22 divisions of multis; 24 of the former and 7 of the latter reported that they had no information about industrial actions at their establishments.
( ) number of occasions.

2.011 Picketing and blacking reported at 100 multi-establishment
manufacturing companies and divisions of companies in 1979*

	Companies and divisions		Employees	
	Number	Per cent	Number	Per cent
No experience of industrial action of any kind	18	18.0	21,717	2.7
Internal stoppages of work, including those arising out of own industry disputes:	62	62.0	606,470	76.7
of which picketing took place in	42	67.7	472,430	77.9
Picketing arising out of 'unrelated' disputes	34	34.0	318,294	40.2
Affected by picketing in connection with disputes:				
involving suppliers	8	8.0	137,528	17.4
involving customers	2	2.0	32,502	4.1
Affected by blacking of goods:				
in	8	8.0	137,029	17.3
out	7	7.0	99,792	12.6
All companies and divisions	100	100.0	791,052	100.0

* CBI Survey: 102 multi-establishment companies and 29 divisions of
   multis *less* 24 MECs and 7 divisions which had no information on
   industrial action at their establishments.

2.012 Industrial action and picketing reported by 100 multi-
establishment companies and divisions of companies in 1979*

	Companies		Occasions	
	Number	Per cent	Number	Per cent
Withdrawals of labour	71	71.0	824	78.3
Overtime bans	67	67.0	125	11.9
Go-slows etc.	38	38.0	67	6.4
Blacking-in	8	8.0	21	2.0
Blacking-out	7	7.0	15	1.4
Any internal action	78	78.0	1,052	100.0
Picketing:				
own dispute	25	25.0	40	31.5
own sympathetic	7	7.0	8	6.3
national dispute	17	17.0	22	17.3
involving suppliers	8	8,0	18	14.2
involving customers	2	2.0	2	1.6
'unrelated'	34	34.0	37	29.1
Any picketing	59	59.0	127	100.0

* Some companies reported picketing of more than one kind.

2.013 Sources of dispute giving rise to picketing at 59 multi-establishment companies and divisions of companies

	Companies	
	Number	Per cent
'Unrelated' only	17	28.8
National - own industry	9	15.2
Own dispute only	7	11.8
Own dispute and 'unrelated'	4	6.8
Own dispute and national	4	6.8
Own dispute, national and 'unrelated'	3	5.1
Own dispute, supplier and 'unrelated'	2	3.4
Supplier and 'unrelated'	2	3.4
Sympathetic and 'unrelated'	2	3.4
Own dispute and sympathetic	2	3.4
Supplier only	1	1.7
Sympathetic and supplier	1	1.7
Own dispute, sympathetic and supplier	1	1.7
Supplier, customer and 'unrelated'	1	1.7
Own dispute, sympathetic and 'unrelated'	1	1.7
National and 'unrelated'	1	1.7
Own dispute, customer and 'unrelated'	1	1.7
All sources	59	100.0

2.014 Claims for unfair dismissal in past five years

| | Multi-establishment cos. | | | | Divisions of multis | | | |
| | Number | | Per cent | | Number | | Per cent | |
	Cos.	Claims	Cos.	Claims	Cos.	Claims	Cos.	Claims
No claims	22	–	21.6	–	10	–	34.5	–
Subject to claims	80	–	78.4	–	19	–	65.5	–
of which:								
1 only	10	10	12.6	0.8	3	3	15.8	3.7
2	12	24	15.0	2.0	5	10	26.4	12.5
3	10	30	12.6	2.5	2	6	10.5	7.5
4	5	20	6.2	1.6	0	0	0.0	0.0
5	5	20	6.2	1.6	2	10	10.5	12.5
6	2	12	2.5	1.0	4	24	21.0	30.0
7	1	7	1.2	0.6	1	7	5.3	8.8
8	3	24	3.7	2.0	0	0	0.0	0.0
9 and more	23	1,072	28.8	87.9	2	20	10.5	25.0
No response	9	–	11.2	0.0	0	0	0.0	0.0
	80	1,219	100.0	100.0	19	80	100.0	100.0

	Multi-establishment cos.	Divisions of multis
Average number of claims per company or division:		
N = total	11.9	2.8
N = subject to claims	15.2	4.2

	Number	Per cent	Number	Per cent
Companies and divisions noting sources of difficulty:*				
conciliation procedure	11	7.7	1	3.4
preparation time	58	40.8	16	55.2
time spent at tribunal	44	31.0	6	20.8
amount of award	3	2.1	1	3.4
press publicity	9	6.3	2	6.9
other difficulty	17	12.1	3	10.3
	142	100.0	29	100.0

*Some companies gave more than one difficulty.

3 The staffing of employee relations

The background

'Employee relations specialists' had their origins in appointments made by companies in the nineteenth century to take care of the welfare of employees and in the expanded demand for facilities to deal with such matters during the first great war of 1914-1918. Some such appointments survived the inter-war depressions. A new phase of development was stimulated by the second world war which produced an added load of labour administration in Essential Work Orders, joint consultation and negotiation; thus, in the words of Gerald Moxon, Personnel Director of United Glass and a leading authority on the subject at that time, 'replacing the patronising and welfare of earlier years by a more fundamental principle of personnel management wider in scope and more technical in application' than previously.

The extent of employee relations specialisms in Britain remains, despite continued pressures for development, difficult to assess. The Institute of Personnel Management has upwards of 20,000 members, but many practising specialists, with or without professional qualifications, do not appear among them. Over the years the services offered have widened and risen in the hierarchy of management, encompassing work study, training, health and safety and manpower planning as well as consultation, negotiation and personnel administration and now including specialist executives and directors at divisional and headquarters as well as works levels. But little information is available on how such specialists are distributed within companies or why or when they were appointed.

More important even than these considerations is the fact that, having divested itself of its welfare image to a considerable extent, personnel management has for some time seemed uncertain of its role. There has existed, and still exists in some quarters, the view that specialisation in employee relations involves the application of a 'normative' set of policies and practices to which all organisations ought to aspire in developing their management/employee relationships and which it is the duty of employee relations specialists to urge upon other managers. Many standard works on personnel practice appear to recommend such an approach to their readers. Textbooks on general management, by contrast, tend to take a different approach, eschewing the possible existence of professional standards and seeing employee relations as subordinate to whatever corporate strategy management may care to develop in the interest of the business, or, in some instances as a 'soft veneer' which exists mainly to reduce resistance to the application of such strategies.

In an attempt to throw light on the dilemmas for employee relations specialists in identifying their role in industry, recent studies of the situation have tended to describe this either as 'diagnostic problem solving' or simply as 'contingent' on 'specific organisational require-ments and circumstances'. Adoption of these approaches implies that specialists, while they may be 'professional' in the sense that they employ specialised information and techniques, are primarily concerned to match these to circumstances over which they have incomplete control and that they are, by the very nature of their function, 'organisation men' rather than apostles of justice and good practice.

Associated with these notions are a number of observations which are currently expressed, either as a matter of opinion or on the basis of evidence on the present condition of employee relations specialisation. First, there is the belief held by many managers that specialists have failed (if this was ever their intention) to secure for themselves a unique function in employee relations management and that this remains to a considerable (or even an overwhelming) extent in the hands of the line and staff managers in charge of factories and departments, with specialists acting in an advisory rather than an executive capacity. Second, there is evidence that, within this general situation, there are considerable variations in the role and function of specialists from company to company and from factory to factory within the same company and that only in a limited number of instances have multi-establishment concerns developed a neat, tidy and uniform system common to all their establishments. Thirdly, it is widely held that employee relations specialists have penetrated only slowly into the boardrooms of companies and that their influence on policy making is relatively weak, especially as a result of their absence from *main* boards of British enterprises.

The survey throws light on some of these questions. The principal points which appear to emerge are summarised at the end of this section; the data speaks for itself. One caveat may be entered in advance. It would be an error to suppose that in the case of most companies in the survey there can be said to exist an 'establishment', or 'complement' of managers and functions in the military or civil service sense which companies are committed or concerned to maintain in staffing their employee relations (or other) activities. The initial deployment of employee relations managers or executives is often experimental and sometimes unsuccessful. The approach of companies to subsequent development is often cautious and many remain uncommitted to any particular pattern of organisation or staffing, thinking it proper and prudent to be free to change this as personalities and situations alter. During the course of our inquiries, several of the companies involved changed their views of what was required in current circumstances.

Single establishment companies

It might be supposed that, if only on grounds of size and relatively undifferentiated management functions, single establishment companies would make only modest use of employee relations specialists. This is indeed the case. Of the 156 companies covered by the survey only 24 (or 15 per cent) had such a manager (3.9a). Twenty-one of these employed one 'personnel', 'industrial relations' or similar manager only; three had more than one, the second being a deputy of some kind. In all but a few cases the post of employee relations manager (under whatever title), had been created within the last 20 years (3.9b). Two-thirds of the posts had been created since 1965, numbers having increased most dramatically between the Industrial Relations Act 1971 and the Employment Protection Act 1975. The increase in numbers appeared, at the time of the survey, likely to continue at a modest rate. Three companies reported that they had recently abandoned the employment of an employee relations specialist; five were contemplating an appointment for the first time.

Size was the reason most often given for *not* having an employee relations manager. 'The company is not large enough for such a post'; 'the workforce is too small'. Those companies which had taken the decision to appoint had it seems, very different ideas about what size was appropriate. Four such companies had between 90 and 100 employees; the rest were to be found in every size group between 100 and 2,000 plus. Taking such a step was, as some unconvinced companies pointed out, as much a question of management style as lack of numbers. 'We try to keep matters on a direct, personal basis'; 'the directors are in close touch with employees'; 'each manager must be his own employee relations/personnel manager as far as possible'; 'we believe that the present management is quite capable of handling the situation'.

Variations on these themes appeared to underlie the employee relations staffing policies of all companies. The principal choices appeared to be three. Firstly, companies could take the view that responsibility for employee relations, both logically and practically, rests with *everyone*. Thus no *one* manager (or supervisor) is specifically responsible; *all* have responsibility: 'we all work together for the benefit of company employees'. About 3 in 10 of the survey companies adopted this stance (3.9a). Although almost one-half of them employed fewer than 50 people, not all were so small. One in six employed more than 250; the largest had over 800; the average labour force represented was just over 130.

A second choice is to treat employee relations primarily as a departmental or functional responsibility, each department or function conducting day-to-day relationships as it thinks best. 'The company is well departmentalised; each manager/foreman is responsible for his own staff; this works quite well.' Almost 20 per cent of the single establishment companies in the survey characterised their arrangements in this way. They were mostly small, ranging in size from 14 to 226 employees, with an average of 70.

The largest group of companies – almost 36 per cent – adopted a third choice, that of giving general responsibility for employee relations at management level to a single manager. 'In a company of this size the job must be carried out by a responsible person, namely the works manager.' 'The most responsible manager' varied from company to company (3.9a), but was most frequently the most senior line manager or a specialist employee relations manager under one title or another – personnel, industrial relations, personnel services etc. – in about one-third of the cases, sometimes with the assistance of another departmental specialist (e.g. a company secretary) to deal with staff as distinct from manual workers, or *vice versa*. Companies adopting this method varied in size from 12 employees to 2,150, with an average of about 260. Personnel managers had, on the average, larger companies under their day-to-day supervision – about 580 employees – than production or works managers, 'constituencies' of about 100.

The small proportion of employee relations managers in the survey companies reflects a clear preference that such matters should be regulated and controlled by line managers where practicable. Having appointed a specialist, the companies do not, however, think of him as *executive*, except within his immediate delegated competence. On the other hand, they do not, for the most part, appear to see him as responsible to *another manager*.

The first of these points can be illustrated from Table 3.10. Very few companies thought of an employee relations function as relieving line management of all its employee responsibilities; two-thirds saw it as primarily advisory. Some 28 per cent continued to think of it as performing an 'intermediary' or 'honest broker' role between company and employees, a view once widely held among personnel managers, but less popular today. Most of the 44 companies which supported this view were expressing theory rather than practice, since they themselves had no personnel staff. Seven of those with employee relations specialists were, however, numbered among them. They were by no means, by the size standards of the group, small, varying in size from 100 to 726 employees, with an average of 374 compared with the average of all those holding this view of the personnel function of 142. It may be of interest that this view should continue to be so widely held, reflecting, as it seems to do, a degree of paternalism not nowadays thought to be acceptable.

Examination of the reporting relationships of personnel specialists involves consideration of how the boards of the companies appear to see their employee relations functions. 'I suppose', noted one chairman/managing director with 40 employees, 'that I am a one man band.' In very few of the companies was functional activity, on paper at least, so highly concentrated. Most had between one and five active directors[1] of three kinds: supervision/general (e.g. chairmen, managing directors etc.), 41 per cent of all directors; works and production, almost 20 per cent; marketing/sales, 17 per cent; finance, 8 per cent and technical, 4 per cent. In about two-fifths of the companies, *none* of these directors was recognised as having *primary* employee relations responsibility (3.2a), but most functions relating to it are evidently in most cases carried on piecemeal by chairman, managing director or works or production director; in others they are more widely scattered over available board members (3.5). Six out of ten, however, recognise one director as being primarily in charge. In these cases, there is an even higher concentration on general managing and production directors who take responsibility in 84 per cent of cases (3.2a).

In companies of this kind, personnel directors feature but little. Six such directors were identified, of whom four were said to have primary responsibility. In practice, this understated the situation since it has clearly become the policy of some companies to employ directors with dual experience, one of them being in employee relations, combining

1 See Table 4.1, p.107.

this with the job of company secretary or production or managing director. In some cases this may be the result of skills and experience acquired *within* the company; in others such skill and experience may have been acquired elsewhere. Among other situations an interesting development has begun to arise in which a manager initially trained for personnel has become a general or works manager, and subsequently the combined managing/personnel or production/personnel director of another company. That such jobs are, in the minds of the holders, easily combined where time is concerned, is evident from Table 3.2b. One director only was regarded as full-time, 10 per cent only worked at employee relations more than half-time, though in the quarter of all 98 cases in which there was a director recognised as having employee relations responsibilities, the time spent was said to be increasing.

The responsibility situation at company board level provides the basis for the reporting relationships of personnel managers, where these exist. Where there is a personnel director there may be no personnel manager in single establishment companies, since this may appear merely to duplicate the function. Most personnel managers, therefore, report to managing directors or production directors. They are only infrequently regarded as regular members of board executive committees (four out of 24 cases) or as occasional members (three out of 24). Only in one case did a personnel manager report to a personnel director. The status of such managers seems, therefore, to be an intermediate one - advisory, not responsible to a fellow manager, but directly so to an individual director. And, if they are to accept such an individual, companies prefer, as with personnel directors, experience and understanding of their problems - personnel managers with experience in the central personnel division of a large company, with experience as a factory manager, a former departmental manager with knowledge of a particularly sensitive area of the company's employee relations, and so on.

In single establishment companies the position of employee relations can perhaps be summarised as follows. Companies prefer to handle matters informally between managers or on a departmental basis but tend towards allocating board responsibility part-time to a particular director, usually a managing or a production director, and occasionally make specific appointments of directors knowledgeable on employee relations matters, whether designated as personnel directors or not. Employee relations specialists at management level tend, for preference, to be of a similar kind but are only employed at all after considerable thought and in circumstances which seem to make them clearly necessary. The issue may be one of cost, either of grounds of size and turnover or because such a manager is thought of as an *on cost* rather than as a member of management making a direct contribution to profitability. But the employment of employee relations managers may seem undesirable on other grounds. Companies frequently refer to the importance of *personal* relations between managers and employees and to the need for all managers to maintain such relations. Where this feeling is strong there is a tendency to think that a 'third party' may complicate the situation and that such an appointment is in some sense an acknowledgement of failure. There may also be, if an employee relations appointment is made as a result of employee organisation or because of a need to deal with legislative change, a feeling of caution about the role that a personnel manager may perform in acknowledging the effective presence of these factors in the situation. Nevertheless, the use of specialists appears to be on the increase.

Where the incidence of employee relations directors and managers is concerned it might be supposed that the presence of trade unions would be associated with the presence of such specialists and that they would occur less frequently in non-union establishments. The survey suggests that this is not overwhelmingly so. Of the 93 companies with trade unions about three-quarters had no such director or manager while this was so in 9 out of 10 of the non-union firms (3.3). Almost 60 per cent of the unionised firms did not negotiate with those unions; of those that did, about one-half had an employee relations director or manager. Negotiation was most likely however in that group of companies which had *both* unions and responsible managers or directors - in 70 per cent of the cases (3.4).

Establishments of multis

The establishments of multi-establishment companies in the survey were on the average larger than the single establishment companies in numbers employed and included a very substantial proportion of foreign owned enterprises. Thirty-three per cent employed fewer than 100 employees, compared with 57 per cent in the case of single establishment companies, while one-third employed more than 500 compared with one-tenth. Of the 125 addresses identifying themselves as 'establishments of multis' in our original questionnaire, 62 per cent declared themselves to be wholly or parly foreign owned. Those returning the second question-naire replied in almost exactly the same proportion — 59 per cent foreign owned.

As already noted, the significance of this balance of replies is far from clear. It may be that CBI membership has particular attractions for companies of this kind. In practice such foreign owned subsidiaries did not think of themselves as unusual from the employee relations point of view. In most cases they considered themselves to be completely autonomous and there was little evidence to the contrary in their responses generally. Almost all had a board or management committee, though there were a few which followed the 'branch factory' system and some which, like some single establishment companies, were 'one man bands', operating with a single director only. The size range of the establishments varied as widely as that of single establishment companies, the smallest having under 20 workers and the largest over 2,000.

An immediately obvious difference between 'individual establishments' and 'single establishments' is the tendency of the former to employ more employee relations managers and hence to leave matters less to works and production managers and managing directors alone. Almost 6 out of 10 have such managers compared with half that figure in single establishment companies. It seemed to make very little difference whether the establishment was UK or foreign owned. Size may have had a hand in the situation, but the same variation in 'size perception' of need (or otherwise) seems to occur in both singles and establishments of multis. One of the latter thought a personnel manager necessary for 57 employees; another employing 2,000 and more considered his enterprise 'too small'!

A clear difference between the two groups is the less evident tendency of the individual establishment of the multi to regard employee relations as the concern of no *one* person or group (15 per cent compared with 30 per cent) or as primarily a departmental responsibility (9 per cent compared with 13 per cent). Perhaps the main distinction is that, in establishments of multis, the 'proprietorial' air tends to predominate in fewer cases and the 'managerial' in more. This would not be out of line with the thought that family owned or traditionally run single establishment companies have, on acquisition, ceased to be 'independent' and have become open to different pressures of managerial style.

This is borne out by the higher proportion of directors (or management committee members) designated as 'personnel', 'personnel services' or in one case 'administration and manpower'. These were identified in ten (30 per cent) of the companies, compared with six (4 per cent) in single establishment concerns. This was not because there was a higher proportion of directors in the former who were recognised as having primary responsibility for employee relations. This proportion remained about the same (61 per cent compared with 63 per cent). The conclusion appears to be the obvious one - that as ownership and control became less personal and more professional, the tendency to specialism increases, though not in all cases. While it becomes less easy to say, 'we don't need [an employee relations specialist], we don't allow such problems to occur', not all companies acquiring others have any wish to alter personalities or style until this becomes necessary as a result of retirements and other eventualities. Newly appointed directors themselves may not wish for such a change if an old style is personally acceptable to them and still working to advantage. There is also, as in the case of single establishment companies, the tendency to appoint non-employee relations directors with employee relations experience and expertise acquired at other companies - 'our production director had a group personnel function in his previous company'.

Further situations appear which are alien to single establishment companies. A director of industrial relations can have been acquired from group personnel staff; a personnel manager can be shared between two establishments of the same company. Individual establishments of multis can command resources which single establishment companies lack. Nevertheless, at director level, employee relations is still commonly a part-time affair, even for those with employee relations titles (3.2b) and the pressure of work to increase is also acknowledged. Specifically appointed directors in employee relations tended to be introduced a little earlier in time (3.2c) and there is some evident change in style in the reported fact that relatively few continue to think of the employee relations function as relieving line management of all employee responsibilities or simply as an acceptable intermediary between employees and management, with a consequently greater emphasis on its advisory role (3.10). Individual establishments of multis would, of course, on the findings of this survey, claim to be less 'paternalistic' than singles (8.3); they are also somewhat more likely to recognise trade unions (about 70 per cent compared with 60 per cent). It is a matter for speculation whether employee relations specialists are a response to trade unionism or whether, as many respondents among single establishment companies suggested, that they also contribute towards trade union development because of their professionalism.

In either event, specialists seemed at the time of the survey to be on the increase, if not necessarily at the rapid rate of the early 1970s and, while the trend towards recognising *a* director (whether 'personnel' or otherwise) as responsible for employee relations seemed likely to continue, four out of ten companies, whether single establishment or establishment of multi, continued to distribute responsibility over directors generally rather than suggesting that one director was overall in control (3.5).

Headquarters and divisions of multi-establishment companies

In multi-establishment companies three main levels exist at which employee relations staffing may be required – at headquarters, at the level of any constituent company, group or division, and at the level of any production or trading establishment. In practice the situation does not necessarily involve all three such levels. Some multi-establishment companies have no 'divisional organisation'. There were 14 instances in the survey (almost 14 per cent) in which this was the case. Others have 'mixed' organisations, some parts being divisionalised and others consisting of establishments reporting directly to head office. Where there are divisions some may act, so far as employee relations are concerned, entirely independently of head office and report to it on specified financial matters only; in other cases the relationship may vary from a situation of complete subordination to the loosest advisory one. Such variations may be repeated in the case of individual production or trading establishments.

At company headquarters the situation can also be complex. A relatively small number have a highly centralised style of employee relations management, most substantial decisions being made at head office. A larger number adopt a more 'articulated' style reflecting the extent of independence given to divisions or establishments. Main boards may prefer to remain distant from executive employee relations decisions or to become more closely involved in them. They may or may not have 'executive' or 'management' committees, the membership of which may consist either of more prominent board members or have some connection with constituent divisions, businesses or establishments. Employee relations representation on such boards or committees, whether in the form of directors or non-board executives, varies from one company to another. Some main boards seek to have no *direct* influence on employee relations at all.[1] In these cases the distinction made in our original questionnaire between the headquarters of a company with employee relations functions and that of a holding company for financial purposes only becomes a somewhat tenuous one.

In the tables which follow the figure '102' represents the total of the companies responding to our second questionnaire as 'headquarters of multi-establishment companies with subsidiary groups, divisions, businesses and establishments'. Since many similar questions were asked of 'groups, divisions or companies' or multis, the 29 of these can sometimes be added to 102 to make 131, the difference being made up of the respondent 'divisions'. Where a total of 125 appears, 6 companies have been deducted from this 131 figure, these being companies with no headquarters in the UK.

1 It is hardly possible to escape the thought that there are few board decisions of any significance which have *no* employee relations implication at all, if only of an indirect kind.

Companies with full-time employee relations directors on main boards

Twenty-six of the 102 multi-establishment companies, with a total of 441,000 employees (i.e. rather more than one-quarter) reported a full-time employee relations director on their main board. Few of them employed less than 1,000 workers, with an average for all of 17,000.[1] An additional three main board directors featured in the divisional returns (3.01a to c). Mostly they were known as 'personnel directors', but others bore such titles as 'employee relations director', 'director of industrial relations', 'head of personnel' or some variant upon them. In almost all cases they reported to the chairman or managing director (019.2(1)). One company had two co-equal directors, one for industrial relations and one for personnel, but in no other company were collective bargaining and personnel administration so clearly distinguished. In all other instances the single director appeared to take overall responsibility for *all* employee relations functions, however he might segregate these in allocating them to the subordinate employee relations staff which all had and controlled. Eighteen per cent of companies reported that they made no such distinction at headquarters level and hardly more than 20 per cent at divisional and establishment levels (3.05).

Almost all the main board posts were of recent creation. Fifteen of them were said to have been established since the middle 1970s; only 5 were older than 1960 (3.02c). All but one were represented as being posts which would be refilled if the present incumbent resigned or retired. This was an assumption which we had reason to question in some cases. One of the companies concerned no longer has a full-time main board employee relations director, and others may be in like case. One reason for this is the evident absence in many of them of a well-established employee relations hierarchy of specialists which can serve to maintain both itself and its succession, with ultimate accession to the main board as the crown and reward of a successful professional career. About one half of the survey companies appeared to fall into this category. The other half seemed less committed to a full-time specialist on their main board. In some it seems likely that *ad hominem* appointments had been made, either as a reward for individual service or because a particular need had arisen which seemed to suggest that a particular personality, often transferred from works management, would be a useful addtion to the board in an employee relations capacity (3.02a and b). A number of these appointments brought with them employee relations experience of a practical kind which, in principle at least, they could have supplied without main board membership.

1 A Korn/Ferry survey taken in the same year showed 30 per cent of a sample of *Times 1000* companies to have a main board executive personnel director. These companies were on average larger than the present sample (see Lindsay, 1981).

However this may be, the companies gave as much credit to such experience as they appeared to give to professional qualifications and were clearly inclined to use the 'home grown' product rather than import talent from outside. Less than one-quarter of full-time employee relations main board directors had been recruited on the open market. One of the posts so created is known subsequently to have disappeared in a board room reshuffle; in another the specialist concerned is evidently valued for his directorial capacities in subsidiary companies and seems to be used more and more in this capacity. The expression 'full-time' in employee relations may not in all cases represent the true position of many of the incumbents noted in the survey. For practical purposes it may be difficult to determine where 'employee relations' begins and ends. While we can readily recognise 'welfare', 'health and safety', 'medical', 'training' and similar matters as falling within employee relations, can we say the same of 'HQ administration', 'management services' and 'public relations'? And what are we to understand when an employee relations director has 'general board duties', is the chairman of a subsidiary company, is in charge of overseas or European subsidiaries or looks after 'certain technical matters'? It may be that main board membership in some cases demands a willingness to devote time and attention to more than a single predominant interest where employee relations are concerned and that companies, in making appointments, are tending to have regard to the willingness and ability of the appointee to establish himself as a contributor to the management and resolution of other matters than those apparent in his title or immediate concerns.

Whether this is so or not, there is no suggestion from the survey that main board employee relations directors are being restricted in their access to the inner counsels of their companies, or denied assistants to enable them to pay detailed attention to their employee relations tasks. Wherever there was an 'inner cabinet' in the survey companies (in almost 40 per cent of the cases) the employee relations director was reported to be a member (3.02c). His assistants were in all cases numerous and ranged through the whole gamut of job titles for employee relations staff - 'personnel', 'industrial relations', 'wages', 'salaries', 'remuneration', 'manpower planning', 'recruitment', 'training', 'welfare', 'health', 'safety', 'security', 'medical', etc.

Companies with main board directors with part-time responsibility for employee relations

Thirty-one of the 102 multi establishment companies in the survey reported that they had on their main board a director recognised as having responsibility for employee relations, but either combining this responsibility with another function as part of his 'job description' or performing it as a 'sideline' of his principal designated activity. The latter greatly exceeded the former in numbers, being mostly chairmen, managing directors, chief executives, production directors, general managers, but with a scattering of administration directors spending less than a quarter of their time on employee relations matters, but in two cases about one-half, and in one case, three-quarters (3.03). 'Shared function' directors who specifically combined responsibilities in the job titles included a 'director trading and personnel', a 'director personnel and Europe' and an 'executive director fluid power group/ executive director personnel'. Both groups included names well-known and distinguished in the employee relations scene, but most were not known in that capacity.

Some major companies featured in the list of those with part-time main board employee relations directors. On the whole they were smaller than those having full-time employee relations directors. Their average number of employees was 8,300 compared with 17,000. But they nevertheless included several employing between 30,000 and 50,000. One reported that it had had a full-time director in the past, two that they would very likely appoint one in the future. The reasons for adopting a part-time in preference to a full-time situation may in some cases involve considerations of size, but in others the position may be more complex. There was less evidence here of employee relations professionalism providing hierarchical reasons for a full-time situation and some of the large companies showed the kind of company structures which appear on paper to be so loosely articulated that they appear not to lend themselves readily to the notion of a main board director acting under an employee relations designation. Further detailed inquiry might help to explain the position more clearly.

About one-third of the companies had no senior employee relations staff to assist the part-time director. With one exception these were very small and for all intents and purposes indistinguishable from single establishment companies of similar size. Nearly one half of the larger ones had management or executive committees. No case was found in which employee relations specialists were regular members of such committees, thus confirming the impression gained from companies with full-time employee relations directors that, where board members accept primary responsibility for such matters even their most senior specialists tend to be excluded from the highest level management discussions unless specially invited.

Companies with no main board specialists, full- or part-time, but with senior full-time employee relations executives

A third group of 23 companies employing slightly fewer than 218,000 employees, on average larger than those with part-time specialist directors (almost 10,000 compared with 8,300) and varying in size between 120 and 25,000, had no main board director, but under one title or another employed a full-time senior executive to deal with employee relations, together with staff in many cases. The most common designation was some variation on the theme 'personnel manager/director,' whether of 'company', 'group' or 'division', but some were compound, e.g. group personnel and administration director. In one case a separately registered 'Group Services Ltd.' operated for employee relations purposes and presumably sold its services to its parent company. An additional 12 companies had an executive board or committee. In every case the senior employee relations executive, though not a main board director, was a constituent member of such a committee. Having no main board director may enable the executive professional to have greater access to the inner counsels of the company.

We do not know from any data collected from the survey whether the employee relations executives were recruited from inside or outside their present companies. General observation would suggest that this group above all is likely to be made up of 'personnel professionals' who have learned their trade at lower levels of employee relations specialisation and who think of themselves as mobile for promotion purposes from divisional to head office levels or from one company to another. Some may ultimately be promoted to full-time main board employee relations status or, *via* line experience, may be those who ultimately become main board members with part-time responsibility for the same function.

Companies with no full-time or part-time employee relations main board directors or senior employee relations executives responsible at headquarters

A fourth group of 22 companies employing about 11,500 employees in total, with an average of 524, and varying in size between 38 and 2,151, had no main board director or senior executive responsible for employee relations, though two had a personnel manager in a junior position in their structures. In these companies ultimate responsibility was taken by chairmen and managing directors for the most part, but also production directors and in four cases, 'the whole board' on an as-and-when basis.

Some of these companies bore strong resemblances to single establishment companies and showed indications that their approach to employee relations was similar to that described above in companies of that kind. 'We have to maintain a very close day to day contact with our staff and experience very little trouble with employee relations' reflected the style that 'employee relations is everyone's business'; others adopted the departmental responsibility approach and a third group were companies which advocated the importance of responsibility residing with a senior individual. 'To get the best understanding over the complete spectrum of employee requirements total understanding by a senior executive is essential.'

Small single establishment practice is thus carried into small multi-establishment situations. Some of the companies had developed more than one factory on the same site as the parent company, or relatively near at hand and these, despite their technical distinction as different establishments and registered companies in most instances, were in practice behaving as departments of a single entity. Others had widely scattered establishments, sometimes in the same trade. A few were 'conglomerate' in nature. The device adopted here was to treat each establishment as far as possible as if it had a separate and distinct management and to make each works manager or managing director responsible for his own employee relations, in some cases with no overt co-ordination or constraint of any kind, but in others seeming to apply personalised pressures for common attitudes through influential main board directors supplemented in some cases by common membership of an employers' association.

Most of the 22 companies seemed contented with this situation. Some appeared to be moving cautiously, and perhaps reluctantly, towards a more specialist employee relations arrangement. One was seeking a personnel manager in his mid 30s, with experience, who could act in a head office capacity to provide common information and advice and perhaps, ultimately, adopt a more executive role if his activities and personality proved to be acceptable. It seems likely that many multi-establishment companies, both small and large, have set out on the process of staffing their employee relations in a similar fashion.

No particular considerations of the proper size which would justify such a transition seem to enter into the situation. Need seems to become evident for less arithmetical reasons - the onset of particular problems, the need to relieve a particular senior manager of a burden of work he can no longer carry; the impending retirement of a chairman or managing director whose successor could hardly be expected to possess his employee relations experience and manage without professional help; the need for organisational change to meet new markets and to recruit new types of labour - all these appeared from the survey to relate to the development of employee relations specialisms within companies.

Divisions of multi-establishment companies

To the 29 divisions of multi-establishment companies which responded to our second questionnaire may be added, for some purposes of analysis, information about their divisional arrangements which was provided by the 88 (out of 102) headquarters of multis which had divisions. Since it did not appear practical at the outset to ask such companies for separate details of *every* such division, the data provided was in some senses incomplete. Sometimes, for example, it was requested on a SOME, MOST, ALL, NONE basis, e.g. in asking whether *some, most, all* or *none* of a company's divisions had a board director responsible for employee relations. As a result, although we can say with certainty how many such companies have *no such directors at all,* we cannot say how many divisions in all are involved, nor yet how many directors. With this limitation in mind, the combined situation in 117 companies is as follows.

Rather more than one-quarter had full-time employee relations directors as members of divisional boards or management committees; a somewhat higher percentage (27.4 per cent) had part-time directors; almost 7 per cent had a 'mixed' situation, i.e. *both* full-time and part-time directors on the same board or full-time on some and part-time on others; 4 out of 10 had no responsible director at all. This is not too unlike the main board situation. Like main boards also, those *without* either full-time or part-time directors mostly made employee relations the responsibility of the chairman or managing director and some (less than one-third) had a full-time executive director with staff to support him (3.01a). Like main board full-time employee relations directors, about one-half of their divisional equivalents had been appointed since the middle 1970s, and few appointments were older than 1960 (3.02c) and there was a mixture between inside and outside recruitment including transfer from other non-employee relations functions, with similar emphasis on practical experience rather than professional qualification *per se*. It is a measure of the policy of companies in subordinating employee relations to line management and in encouraging divisional independence that only in a handful of cases were divisional employee relations directors responsible to higher levels than their own board chairmen or managing directors (3.08b). Part-time divisional board directors were said to spend about the same amount of time on employee relations (less than a quarter) as similarly responsible part-time main board directors.

If the main and divisional board situations tend to be strikingly alike so far as employee relations staffing is concerned it may simply be that in the course of growth by expansion or acquisition, that companies have extended their own staffing habits and those of the businesses acquired, into higher levels of their organisations. While some may have reviewed their structures from head office and sought to regularise their staffing pattern on a common basis, many have simply accepted the pattern as they found it, thinking it best, perhaps, to let sleeping dogs lie. Considered in administrative terms the result is, therefore, somewhat untidy.

Some aspects of this can be seen from Tables 3.04a to d. At main board level 82 directors responsible for employee relations could be identified in 131 companies. Of these companies, almost 14 per cent had a full-time main board director only and 13 per cent a part-time main board director only, while 11 per cent had executive board or management committee directors only, the remaining 61 per cent either having no main board employee representation at all (41 per cent) or being mixed between the two boards.

If divisional boards are included in the description, the situation becomes even more complex (3.04d) for there are in addition companies with representation on main and divisional boards only, full-time and part-time (12.2 per cent), on subsidiary (or management committee) and divisional boards only (8.4 per cent) and on a mixture between all three (10.8 per cent), the total number of identifiable directors of both kinds being 160. The number of directors at *headquarters* tends to increase somewhat by size (3.09b). No company employing over 30,000 employees had no main or subsidiary board director; on an average of 11 companies, they had precisely one. Not all companies employing between 1,000 and 30,000 had such directors (though 15 of these had senior employee relations executives) but 42 out of 51 had main board directors of one kind or the other responsible for employee relations (an average of 0.75 to 0.84 of a director to each company!). Taking large companies with divisions into account, directors existed in substantially all, at one level or another (3.09e).

Establishments of multi-establishment companies

How many of the 2,950 establishments have full-time employee relations staff it is impossible to say. A number of points can, however, be made about that staff and about its relations with line management. The first is that in over 70 per cent of multi-establishment companies and divisions it is the most senior line manager rather than the personnel specialist manager which is regarded as having *general* responsibility for employee relations (3.09a). This percentage falls somewhat in the case of larger companies employing more than 1,000 employees (3.09c) to rather more than one-half and falls to 62 to 65 per cent in companies with full-time main board directors or senior full-time employee relations executives not on the main board, but is higher than average where there are part-time directors or no directors at all (81 to 86 per cent). The situation is substantially the same where day-to-day employee relations are concerned (3.09d). In the over-whelming majority of companies the ultimate control of relationships at establishment level is considered to rest with line management. This seems to be significantly less so where full-time specialists occupy the highest positions in companies.

Summary

1 There is evidence of a considerable increase in employee relations personnel at all levels, especially since the middle 1970s and some indication that this was, at the time of the survey, likely to continue though at a more modest rate.

2 This growth has followed no uniform pattern in the use of employee relations specialists. Companies have tended to develop cautiously, empirically, and with no intention of upsetting the traditional functions and authority of line management in dealing with employees.

3 Despite a continuing preference for men with line experience to assume more specialist employee relations responsibilities both at establishment and at higher levels in companies, there has been a tendency for more 'professional' specialists to make their mark in line appointments and, as a result of such experience, to find their way into boards of companies, sometimes in a full-time and some-times in a part-time role.

4 As a result of these movements, few major multi-establishment companies employing more than 5,000 employees are now likely to be without a main board director with head office responsibility for employee relations, together with a specialised staff, and, in many instances, with divisional directors and staff also.

5 The appointment of employee relations at such high levels in companies seems to have been made acceptable, not only by the promotion of line managers with employee relations experience, but also by the willingness of more 'professional' specialists to acquire line management skills, to adapt themselves to the climate and

behaviour of boards and to contribute to other board activities, including in some cases the management of other functions and constituent companies.

6 The non-board employee relations specialist at head office may acquire considerable influence and even executive authority in companies by membership of executive or management committees of boards, *particularly where no full or part-time main board directors have been given responsibility for employee relations.*

7 Many smaller multi-establishment companies, including those which tend to act primarily as financial holding companies, continue to organise their employee relations along the lines of single establishment companies, some regarding employee relations as the business of everyone and others regarding constituent companies as departments responsible for their own employee relations. There are indications that some companies of this kind are experiencing a need for greater central direction which may ultimately lead to the deployment of employee relations specialisms at head office. Indeed, this appears to be one way in which the present situation generally has evolved.

8 Individual establishments of multi-establishment companies, perhaps because of the emphasis placed by most companies of this kind on maintaining the pre-eminent position of line management in the conduct of employee relations tend to behave and to see themselves as behaving, very much upon the traditional lines of single establishment companies.

9 As a matter of employee relations style, pressures of various kinds, of which the growth of trade unionism is only one, which have encouraged companies to adopt more specialist approaches to employee relations, have resulted in a blend of line management authority with specialist advice and executive skills which each company has been compelled to accept, though with greater or lesser success.

References

Drucker, Peter, *The Practice of Management,* Mercury Books, 1961.

Eaton, Jack, Gill, Colin R. and Morris, Richard S. 'The staffing of industrial relations management in the chemical industry', *Chemistry and Industry,* 17 September 1977.

Guest, David and Horwood, Robert, *The Role and Effectiveness of Personnel Managers,* a Preliminary Report, London School of Economics, Department of Industrial Relations, Report No. 1, Oct. 1980.

Heidrick and Struggles, *Profile of the European Personnel Director*, 1976.

Henstridge, John, 'Personnel Management: A Framework for Analysis', *Personnel Review*, Vol. 4, No. 2, 1975.

Legge, Karen, *Power, Innovation and Problem Solving in Personnel Management*, McGraw-Hill, 1978.

Lindsay, G., *Boards of Directors Study 1981*, Korn/Ferry International, 1981.

Marsh, A.I.,'The staffing of industrial relations management in the Engineering Industry', *Industrial Relations Journal*, Vol. 2, No. 2, 1971.

Marsh, A.I. and Gillies, J.G., 'Involvement of Line and Staff Managers in Industrial Relations', Paper to *SSRC Seminar, Cumberland Lodge*, December 1977.

Moxon, G.R., *The Growth of Personnel Management in Great Britain during the War 1939-45*, Institute of Personnel Management, 1945.

Nichols, T. and Beynon, H. *Living with Capitalism, Class Relations and the Modern Factory*, Routledge and Kegan Paul, 1977.

Poole, M., 'A back seat for personnel', *Personnel Management*, Vol. 5, No. 5 1973.

Rubenowitz, S., 'Personnel Management Organisation in some European Societies', *Management Information Review*, Vol. 8, Special Issue, No. 4, 1968.

Thomason, George F., *A Textbook of Personnel Management*, Institute of Personnel Management, 1976.

Thomason, George F., 'Corporate Control and the Professional Association,' in Michael Poole and Roger Mansfield (eds.), *Managerial Roles and Industrial Relations*, Gower, 1980.

Thurley, Keith and Guest, David, 'Personnel Management: Choice of Strategies for the Enterprise', Paper to the Fifth World Congress of the *International Industrial Relations Association*, 3-7 September 1979.

Tyson, Shaun J.J., *Specialists in Ambiguity: Personnel Management as an Occupation*,(unpublished Ph.D. Thesis, University of London).

Tyson, Shaun J.J., 'The Study of Personnel Management as an Occupation: Research Notes', *Paper to SSRC Seminar*, Cumberland Lodge, December 1977.

Watson, T.J., *The Personnel Managers*, Routledge and Kegan Paul, 1977.

Tabulations

The staffing of employee relations

3.1 Principal functions of active directors

	Single establishment company		Individual establishment multi	
	Number	Per cent	Number	Per cent
Chairman	56	35.9	24	44.4
Chairman/MD	34	21.8	10	18.5
Managing director	96	61.5	32	59.3
Joint/deputy MD	41	26.3	16	29.6
Production/works D.	108	69.2	26	48.1
Marketing/sales D.	92	58.9	26	48.1
Personnel	6	3.8	10	18.5
Finance	43	27.6	24	44.4
Technical	23	14.7	22	40.7
Company secretary	18	11.5	5	9.3
Administrative	6	3.8	5	9.3
Non-executive director	3	1.9	8	14.8
Other	21	13.5	41	75.9
	547*		249*	

* A few companies did not specify the role of each director.

3.2a Director recognised as having primary responsibility for employee relations

	Single establishment company		Individual establishment multi	
	Number	Per cent	Number	Per cent
Recognised director	98	62.8	33	61.1
of which:				
chairman or MD	58	59.2	13	39.4
works or production director	24	24.5	5	15.1
finance	6	6.1	1	3.0
personnel	4	4.1	10	30.4
marketing/sales	2	2.0	0	0.0
technical	1	1.0	2	6.1
administration	0	0.0	1	3.0
company secretary	0	0.0	1	3.0
other director	3	3.1	0	0.0
	98	100.0	33	100.0
of which:				
introduced or appointed to be i/c employee rels.	11	11.2	12	36.4
of which:				
recruited *outside* business	5	45.4	7	58.3
with significant IR experience	5	45.4	10	83.0

3.2b Director recognised as having primary responsibilities for employee relations

	Single establishment company		Individual establishment multi	
	Number	Per cent	Number	Per cent
Recognised director	98	62.8	33	61.1
of which:				
full-time	1	1.0	2	6.1
about three-quarters	2	2.1	2	6.1
about a half	7	7.1	3	9.0
one quarter or less	77	78.6	16	48.5
no response	11	11.2	10	30.3
	98	100.0	33	100.0
for whom:				
time increasing	24	24.5	8	24.2
time decreasing	2	2.0	1	3.1
constant	61	62.3	14	42.4
no response	11	11.2	10	30.3
	98	100.0	33	100.0

3.2c Director recognised as having primary responsibility for
employee relations. Year when job created (specifically
introduced or appointed director)

	Single establishment company		Individual establishment multi	
	Number	Per cent	Number	Per cent
1979	1	9.1	0	0.0
1978	3	27.3	0	0.0
1977	0	0.0	2	16.7
1971-1976	4	36.3	4	33.3
1965-1970	1	9.1	5	41.7
1960-1964	0	0.0	0	0.0
1955-1959	0	0.0	0	0.0
1950-1954	0	0.0	0	0.0
Before 1950	1	9.1	1	8.3
No response	1	9.1	0	0.0
	11	100.0	12	100.0

3.3 Relative incidence of trade unions and directors and managers responsible for employee relations

Single establishment companies with	Responsible board director		Employee relations manager		No employee relations manager		Total
	No.	Per cent	No.	Per cent	No.	Per cent	No.
Trade unions (93 59.6)	3	3.2	20	21.5	70	75.3	93
no trade unions(63 40.4)	1	1.6	5	7.9	57	90.5	63
(156 100.0)	4	2.6	25	16.0	127	81.4	156

3.4 Relative incidence of negotiations and directors and managers responsible for employee relations

Single establishment companies with	Total	Which negotiate	
		Number	Per cent
Both manual and non-manual unions and no ER manager	15	5	33.3
Both manual and non-manual unions and ER manager	12	10	83.3
Both manual and non-manual unions and resp. ER director	3	3	100.0
No unions with responsible ER director	1	-	-
Manual unions and no ER manager	55	14	25.5
Manual unions and ER manager	8	3	37.5
	94	35	37.6

3.5 Distribution of responsibilities for various employee relations matters where no board member has primary responsibility for employee relations

Per cent

	Wage administration S	IE	Salary administration S	IE	Hiring/firing S	IE	Labour planning S	IE	Other companies S	IE	Welfare S	IE	Total matters S	IE
Chairman or managing director(s)	48.8	33.3	60.9	46.7	35.5	46.7	31.7	40.0	57.8	53.3	33.3	40.0	44.1	40.0
Works/production director	7.3	13.3	2.4	–	24.4	13.3	28.6	20.0	5.3	–	21.4	6.7	15.3	8.8
Marketing/sales director	–	–	–	–	2.2	–	2.4	–	–	–	2.4	–	1.2	–
Personnel director	–	13.3	–	20.0	–	20.0	20.0	20.0	–	20.0	–	13.3	–	17.8
Finance director	9.7	6.7	9.7	6.7	4.4	6.7	4.8	20.0	–	–	4.8	–	6.0	6.7
Company secretary	4.9	20.0	4.9	13.3	2.2	–	2.4	–	–	–	2.4	–	2.8	5.5
Admin. director	4.9	6.7	–	–	–	6.7	–	–	–	–	–	6.7	0.8	3.3
Other	24.4	6.7	22.1	13.3	31.3	13.3	11.1	–	36.9	26.7	35.7	33.7	29.8	17.9

3.6 Companies reporting a specific employee relations role for the following managers and executives

	Single establishment company		Individual establishment multi	
	Number	Per cent	Number	Per cent
Production manager or general manager	75	48.1	34	63.0
Company secretary	58	37.1	22	40.7
Sales manager	21	13.5	11	20.4
Senior administrator	20	12.8	8	14.8
Chief accountant	16	10.3	10	18.5
Chief clerk	5	3.2	1	1.9

3.7 Has a philosophy of employee relations

	Single establishment company		Individual establishment multi	
	Number	Per cent	Number	Per cent
	110	70.5	28	51.9

3.8 Distinguishes between industrial relations and personnel management

	Single establishment company		Individual establishment multi	
	Number	Per cent	Number	Per cent
Distinguishes	17	10.9	13	24.1
Does not distinguish	133	84.3	40	74.1
No response	6	4.8	1	1.8
	156	100.0	54	100.0

3.9a Which manager primarily responsible for employee relations?

	Single establishment company		Individual establishment multi	
	Number	Per cent	Number	Per cent
No particular manager	46	29.5	8	14.8
One particular manager	79	50.6	37	68.6
A number of managers	20	12.8	5	9.2
No response	11	7.1	4	7.4
	156	100.0	54	100.0
One particular manager	79	100.0	37	100.0
of which:				
works manager or director	25	31.6	2	5.4
personnel manager	24	30.4	22	59.4
managing director	8	10.1	2	5.4
general manager	7	8.9	3	8.1
production manager	5	6.3	2	5.4
production director	4	5.1	2	5.4
company secretary	3	3.7	2	5.4
administration manager	1	1.3	0	0.0
staff manager	1	1.3	0	0.0
foreman	1	1.3	0	0.0
accountant	0	0.0	1	2.7
technical director	0	0.0	1	2.7

3.9b Employment of employee relations managers. Year in which such a manager first appointed

	Single establishment company		Individual establishment multi	
	Number	Per cent	Number	Per cent
1979	2	8.3	1	4.5
1978	2	8.3	1	4.5
1977	1	4.2	0	0.0
1971–1976	8	33.4	7	31.8
1965–1970	3	12.5	3	13.7
1960–1964	3	12.5	2	9.1
1955–1959	0	0.0	0	0.0
1950–1954	2	8.3	2	9.1
Before 1950	2	8.3	2	9.1
No response	1	4.2	4	19.2
	24	100.0	22	100.0

3.10 General attitude to employee relations function

	Single establishment company		Individual establishment multi	
	Number responses	Per cent companies	Number responses	Per cent companies
Wholly advisory to line management	23	14.7	24	44.4
Executive after consultant with line management	35	22.4	3	5.6
Executive on some matters; advisory on others	56	35.9	16	29.6
To relieve line management of all employee responsibilities	7	4.5	0	0.0
Acceptable intermediaries between employees and management	44	28.2	8	14.8

3.01a Boards having directors with specific or primary responsibility
for employee relations

	Multi* establishment company		Division of multi		Establishment of multi		Single establishment company	
	No.	Per cent	No.	Per cent	No.	Per cent	No.	Per cent
No director responsible	62	49.6	9	31.0	21	38.9	58	37.2
Director responsible:								
full-time **	29	23.2	11***	37.9	2	3.7	1	0.6
part-time	34	27.2	10	31.0	31	57.4	97	62.2
Of part-time main function:								
chairman/MD/ ch. executive	15	44.2	1	10.0	13	41.9	58	59.8
works/production/ general	8	23.6	4	40.0	5	16.1	24	24.7
administration	2	5.9	2	20.0	2	6.5	0	0.0
personnel/pers. services	3	8.9	1	10.0	5	16.1	3	3.1
company secretary	1	2.9	1	10.0	1	3.2	0	0.0
finance	1	2.9	1	10.0	1	3.2	6	6.2
technical	1	2.9	0	0.0	2	6.5	1	1.0
marketing/sales	1	2.9	0	0.0	0	0.0	2	2.1
distribution	1	2.9	0	0.0	0	0.0	0	0.0
other	0	0.0	0	0.0	2	6.5	3	3.1
TOTAL	125*		29		54		156	

* includes 23 HQ boards reported by divisions (6 had no HQ in UK).
** all personnel directors or equivalent function.
*** one division had one full and one part-time director.

3.01b Main and divisional boards having directors specifically
responsible for employee relations

	Multi-establishment companies		Divisions of multis	
	Number	Per cent	Number	Per cent
Boards designating as responsible:				
No director	45	44.1	18 (9)	62.1(31.0)
A part-time director	31	30.4	2 (9)*	6.9(31.0)
A full-time director	26	25.5	3(11)*	10.3(37.9)
No UK board	-	-	6(-)	20.7(-)
	102	100.0	29	100.0

( ) Indicates divisional board.
* One division reported both a full-time and a part-time director
responsible for employee relations.

3.01c Multi-establishment companies: full-time employee relations
executives and managers

	With full-time employee relations executives or managers		Without full-time employee relations executives or managers	
	Number	Per cent	Number	Per cent
With full-time employee relations directors on main boards	26	100.0	0	0.0
With part-time employee relations directors on main boards	21	67.7	10	32.3
With no main board employee relations directors	25	55.6	20	44.4
	72	70.6	30	29.4

3.01d Multi-establishment companies having main board, executive or no headquarters directors responsible for employee relations

Companies with	Number	Per cent	Number of employees	Per cent	Average number employed
Full-time main board director	26	25.5	441,246	47.0	16,971
Part-time main board director	31	30.4	267,700	28.5	8,635
Full-time executive director but no full or part-time main board director	23	22.5	217,864	23.2	9,472
No main board or full-time executive at headquarters	22	21.6	11,536	1.3	524
	102	100.0	938,346	100.0	9,199

3.02a Main and divisional boards with full-time directors responsible for employee relations

	Multi-establishment companies		Divisions of multis	
	Number	Per cent	Number	Per cent
Number with full-time directors	26	100.0	3(11)	100.0(100.0)
of which:				
personnel director	25	96.1	3(7)	100.0(63.6)
other title	1	3.9	0(4)	0.0(36.4)
regarded as permanent post	23	88.5	N.A.(10)	(91.0)
appointed from:				
outside	6	23.1	N.A.(6)	(54.5)
promoted ER function	9	34.6	N.A.(5)	(45.5)
transferred	11	42.3	N.A.(0)	(0.0)
transferred from post as:				
managing director	3	11.5	No	
works director	1	3.8		
works management	3	11.5	information	
other	4	15.4		
with previous experience	10	38.5		
with professional qualifications	12	46.1	3(7)	100.0(63.6)
with other directional functions	18	69.2	2(10)	66.7(91.0)
responsible to:				
chairman	9	34.6	1(1)	33.3(9.0)
managing director	14	53.8	2(10)	66.7(91.0)
board	2	7.7	0(0)	
other	1	3.9	0(0)	

( ) Indicates divisional board.

3.02b Characteristics of full-time main board and divisional employee relations directors

	Multi-establishment companies		Divisions of multis	
	Number	Per cent	Number	Per cent
Number with full-time directors	29	100.0	11	100.0
of which:				
personnel director	28	96.5	7	63.6
other title	1	3.5	4	36.4
regarded as permanent post (N=26 for main boards)	23	88.5	10	91.0
appointed from: (N=26 for main boards)				
outside	6	23.1	6	54.5
promoted ER function	9	34.6	5	45.5
transferred	11	42.3	0	0.0
transferred from post as: (N=11)				
managing director	3	27.3		
works director	1	9.1		
works management	3	27.3		
other	4	36.3		
with previous experience (N=11)	10	91.0		
with professional qualifications (N=29 for main board)	15	51.7	7	63.6
with other directoral functions	20	70.0	10	91.0
responsible to:				
chairman	10	34.5	1	9.0
managing director	16	55.2	10	91.0
board	2	6.9	0	0.0
other	1	3.4	0	0.0

3.02c Main and divisional boards with full-time directors responsible for employee relations

	Multi-establishment companies		Divisions of multis	
	Number	Per cent	Number	Per cent
Number with full-time directors	26	100.0	3 (11)	100.0(100.0)
Year in which specialised full-time function created:				
1979	5	19.3	0 (2)	0.0(18.2)
1978	3	11.6	1 (0)	33.3(0.1)
1977	4	15.4	0 (0)	0.0(0.0)
1971-1976	5	19.3	1 (4)	33.3(36.4)
1965-1970	4	15.4	1 (4)	33.3(36.4)
1960-1964	1	3.8	0 (0)	0.0(0.0)
1955-1959	1	3.8	0 (0)	0.0(0.0)
1950-1954	1	3.8	0 (1)	0.0(9.1)
before 1950	1	3.8	0 (0)	0.0(0.0)
no response	1	3.8	0 (0)	0.0(0.0)
with subsidiary or executive board or management committee	10	38.5		
of which full-time director a member	10	100.0		

( ) Indicates divisional board.

3.02d Year of appointment of full-time directors responsible for employee relations

	Multi-establishment companies		Divisions of multis	
	Number	Per cent	Number	Per cent
Number with full-time directors	29	100.0	11	100.0
Specialised function created:				
1979	5	17.3	2	18.2
1978	4	13.8	0	0.0
1977	4	13.8	0	0.0
1971-1976	6	20.8	4	36.4
1965-1970	5	17.3	4	36.4
1960-1964	1	3.4	0	0.0
1955-1959	1	3.4	0	0.0
1950-1954	1	3.4	1	9.0
before 1950	1	3.4	0	0.0
no response	1	3.4	0	0.0

3.03 Main and divisional boards with part-time directors responsible for employee relations

	Multi-establishment companies		Divisions of multis	
	Number	Per cent	Number	Per cent
Number with part-time directors	31	100.0	2 (10)*	100.0(100.0)
Principal function of part-time director:				
MD/deputy chairman	9	29.1	0 (1)	0.0(10.0)
works/production/general	8	25.9	0 (4)	0.0(40.0)
chief executive	5	16.2	1 (0)	50.0(0.0)
administration	1	3.2	1 (2)	50.0(20.0)
management services	1	3.2	0 (0)	0.0(0.0)
personnel	1	3.2	0 (1)	0.0(10.0)
company secretary	1	3.2	0 (1)	0.0(10.0)
finance	1	3.2	0 (1)	0.0(10.0)
technical	1	3.2	0 (0)	0.0(0.0)
distribution	1	3.2	0 (0)	0.0(0.0)
marketing	1	3.2	0 (0)	0.0(0.0)
no response	1	3.2	0 (0)	0.0(0.0)
Time spent on employee relations:				
more than three-quarters	2	6.5	0 (1)	0.0(10.0)
about one-half	3	9.7	0 (1)	0.0(10.0)
one-quarter or less	25	80.6	2 (8)	100.0(80.0)
no response	1	3.2	0 (0)	0.0(0.0)
Had full-time director in the past	1	3.2	0 (0)	0.0(0.0)
Intend considering full-time director in future	2	6.5	0 (0)	0.0(0.0)

*Including division reporting both a full-time and part-time director responsible for employee relations.
( ) Indicates divisional board.

81

3.04a Multi-establishment companies: full-time and part-time directors with responsibility for employee relations, main and subsidiary boards and divisional boards, by total number of employees

N=102

Total number of employees	Main and subsidiary board directors				Divisional board directors				Boards with no directors	
	Full-time		Part-time		Full-time		Part-time			
	No.	%	No.	%	No.	%	No.	%	No.	%
Less than 50	0	0.0	1	0.0	0	0.0	0	0.0	0	0.0
51-100	0	0.0	4	8.5	0	0.0	2	10.0	4	20.0
101-250	0	0.0	3	6.4	0	0.0	1	5.0	3	15.0
251-500	1	2.0	3	6.4	1	3.4	4	20.0	7	35.0
501-1000	2	4.0	5	10.6	2	6.9	2	10.0	3	15.0
1001-5000	17	34.0	13	27.7	2	6.9	8	40.0	3	15.0
5001-10000	8	16.0	4	8.5	6	20.7	0	0.0	0	0.0
10000-30000	14	28.0	7	14.9	10	34.5	2	10.0	0	0.0
over 30000	7	14.0	5	10.6	8	27.6	0	0.0	0	0.0
no response	1	2.0	2	4.3	0	0.0	1	5.0	0	0.0
	50	100.0	47	100.0	29	100.0	20	100.0	20	100.0

3.04b Multi-establishment companies: main board subsidiary board executive board or management committee directors or members specifically designated as having responsibility for employee relations (102 companies + 29 divisions of companies)

Companies with directors	Number		Per cent	
Full-time on main board only	15	(3)	14.7	(10.3)
Part-time on main board only	16	(1)	15.7	(3.4)
Full-time on subsidiary board only	9	(1)	8.8	(3.4)
Part-time on subsidiary board only	3	(1)	2.9	(3.4)
Full-time both main and subsidiary boards	11	(0)	10.8	(0.0)
Part-time both main and subsidiary boards	12	(1)	11.8	(3.4)
Part-time main board; full-time subsidiary board	4	(0)	3.9	(0.0)
No director, full or part-time	32	(22)	31.4	(76.1)
All companies	102	(29)	100.0	(100.0)

	Directors				Companies	
	Full-time		Part-time			
	Number	Per cent	Number	Per cent	Number	Per cent
Main board only	15 (3)	38.5 (75.0)	16 (1)	45.7 (25.0)	31 (4)	30.4 (13.8)
Subsidiary board only	9 (1)	23.1 (25.0)	3 (1)	8.6 (25.0)	12 (2)	11.7 (6.8)
Both main and subsidiary boards	11 (0)	28.2 (0.0)	12 (2)	34.3 (50.0)	23 (1)	22.6 (3.4)
Part-time main; full-time subsidiary	4 (0)	10.2 (0.0)	4 (0)	11.4 (0.0)	4 (0)	3.9 (0.0)
No director	0 (0)	0.0 (0.0)	0 (0)	0.0 (0.0)	32 (22)	31.4 (76.0)
All companies and directors	39 (4)	100.0 (100.0)	34 (4)		100.0 (100.0)	102 (29) 100.0 (100.0)

( ) Main board directors reported by 29 divisions of multis.

83

3.04c Multi-establishment companies: main board, subsidiary board, executive board or management committee directors or members specifically designated as having responsibility for employee relations

Companies with directors	Number	Per cent
Full-time on main board only	18	13.7
Part-time on main board only	17	13.0
Full-time on subsidiary board only	10	7.6
Part-time on subsidiary board only	4	3.1
Full-time both main and subsidiary boards	11	8.4
Part-time both main and subsidiary boards	13	9.9
Part-time main board; full-time subsidiary board	4	3.1
No director, full or part-time	54	41.2
All companies	131	100.0

| | Directors | | | | Companies | |
| | Full-time | | Part-time | | | |
	No.	Per cent	No.	Per cent	No.	Per cent
Main board only	18	41.8	17	43.6	35	26.7
Subsidiary board only	10	23.3	4	10.2	14	10.7
Both main and subsidiary boards	11	25.6	14	35.9	24	18.3
Part-time main; full-time subsidiary	4	9.3	4	10.3	4	3.1
No director	0		0		54	41.2
All companies and directors	43	100.0	39	100.0	131	100.0

3.04d Multi-establishment companies: main board, subsidiary board, executive board or management committee directors or members and divisional board directors or members specifically designated as having responsibility for employee relations

Companies with directors	Number	Per cent
Full-time on main board only	5	3.8
Part-time on main board only	8	6.1
Full-time on subsidiary board only	4	3.1
Part-time on subsidiary board only	3	2.3
Full-time on divisional board only	13	9.9
Part-time on divisional board only	13	9.9
Full-time main and subsidiary boards only	3	2.3
Part-time main and subsidiary boards only	7	5.3
Full-time subsidiary and divisional boards only	6	4.6
Part-time subsidiary and divisional boards only	0	0.0
Full-time main and divisional boards only	11	8.4
Part-time main and divisional boards only	5	3.8
Full-time main, subsidiary and divisional boards	5	3.8
Part-time main, subsidiary and divisional boards	6	4.6
Full-time main and subsidiary, part-time divisional	3	2.3
Full-time main, part-time divisional only	2	1.5
Part-time main, full-time subsidiary only	4	3.1
Part-time main, full-time divisional only	4	3.1
Part-time subsidiary, full-time divisional only	1	0.8
No director, full or part-time on any board	28	21.3
All companies	131	100.0

| | Directors | | | | Companies | |
| | Full-time | | Part-time | | | |
	No.	Per cent	No.	Per cent	No.	Per cent
Main board only	5	5.6	8	11.3	13	9.9
Subsidiary board only	4	4.5	3	4.2	7	5.4
Divisional board only	13	14.6	13	18.3	26	19.8
Main and subsidiary board only	5	5.6	9	12.7	14	10.7
Subsidiary and divisional only	13	14.6	1	1.4	7	5.4
Main and divisional board only	28	31.5	16	22.5	22	16.8
All boards	21	23.6	21	29.6	14	10.7
No director					28	21.3
All directors and companies	89	100.0	71	100.0	131	100.0

85

3.05 Distinguishes between industrial relations and personnel management

	Multi-establishment companies		Divisions of multis	
	Number	Per cent	Number	Per cent
Distinguishes:				
at company level	18	17.6	6	20.7
at divisional level:				
all divisions	8	7.8	5	17.2
some divisions	15	14.7	1	3.4
at establishment level:				
all establishments	6	5.9	5	17.2
some establishments	15	14.7	1	3.4
of	102		29	

3.06 Main and divisional boards with no director specifically designated as having responsibility for employee relations

	Multi-establishment companies		Divisions of multis	
	Number	Per cent	Number	Per cent
Companies with no director designated as responsible for ERs	45	100.0	18 (9)	100.0 (100.0)
Who takes charge as and when required?				
chairman	5	11.1	2 (0)	11.1 (0.0)
managing director	20	44.4	7 (5)	38.9 (55.5)
the whole board	3	6.7	2 (2)	11.1 (22.2)
another director	14	31.1	6 (0)	33.3 (0.0)
other arrangement	3	6.7	1 (2)	5.6 (22.2)
Companies with senior manager, not on the board who handles ER matters, viz:	41	93.2	(5)	(55.5)
chairman/MD	1	2.4	(0)	(0.0)
personnel director	7	17.2	(0)	(0.0)
personnel manager	19	46.3	(2)	(40.0)
works director	4	9.7	(1)	(20.0)
administration director	1	2.4	(0)	(0.0)
company secretary	2	4.9	(0)	(0.0)
production manager	6	14.7	(1)	(20.0)
other	1	2.4	(1)	(20.0)
	41	100.0	(5)	(20.0)
Of which:				
represents ER function on subsidiary or executive board or management committee	17	41.4	(1)	(20.0)

(no information)

3.07 Subsidiary or executive boards or committees of main or divisional boards dealing with employee relations

	Multi-establishment companies		Divisions of multis	
	Number	Per cent	Number	Per cent
No subsidiary boards dealing with ERs	57	55.9	22	75.9
Subsidiary boards dealing with ERs	43	44.1	3	10.3
No response	2		4	13.8
	102	100.0	29	100.0
Of which: has member specially designated as responsible for ERs	39	90.7	3	100.0
Of which:				
full-time ER	24	61.5	1	0.0
part-time ER	15	38.5	2	66.7
				33.3
Of part-time spent on ER:				
more than three-quarters	2	12.5	0	0.0
about half	4	25.0	1	50.0
a quarter or less	10	62.5	1	50.0
	16	100.0	2	100.0
Of part-time:				
managing director	2	12.5	1	50.0
chief executive	3	18.7	0	0.0
works management	4	25.0	1	50.0
other	7	43.8	0	50.0
Of part-time:				
formerly full-time job	2	12.5	0	0.0
likely to become full-time in future	4	25.0	0	0.0
present incumbent:				
recruited from outside	2	12.5	1	50.0
promoted from ER	3	18.7	0	0.0
from non-ER function	11	68.7	1	50.0
with ER experience	9	56.2	0	0.0

3.08a Subsidiary companies, businesses or divisions of multi-establishment companies

Divisions	Multi-establishment companies	
	Number	Per cent
All divisions	88	86.3
In which a specific board or management committee member has responsibility for ERs:		
all divisions	27	30.7
most divisions	11	12.5
some divisions	12	13.6
No specific board or management committee member has responsibility for ERs	38	43.2
Divisions which include members with specific responsibility	50	56.8
In which members:		
full-time employee relations	20	40.0
part-time employee relations	23	46.0
some part-time; some full-time	7	14.0
If part-time ERs take up:		
more than three-quarters	2	7.7
about one-half	4	15.4
one-quarter or less	17	65.4
no response	3	11.5
	26	100.0
Of which considering full-time appointment	5	19.2
If full-time:		
personnel director	17	58.6
administrative director	1	3.4
personnel manager	8	27.6
other title	3	10.4
	29	100.0

3.08b Subsidiary companies, businesses or divisions of multi-establishment companies

	Multi-establishment companies	
	Number	Per cent
Divisions including full-time members responsible for ERs	29	32.9
Of which posts created:		
1978	4	13.8
1977	4	13.8
1971–1976	6	20.7
1965–1970	7	24.2
1960–1964	2	6.9
1955–1959	1	3.4
1950–1954	0	0.0
Before 1950	2	6.9
no date given	3	10.3
Of which all or some incumbents:		
recruited outside	17	58.6
promoted within ER in company	22	75.9
transferred or promoted from other functions	17	58.6
Of which all or some responsible to:		
higher board chairman/MD	6	20.7
higher board ER director	9	31.0
own board chairman/MD	23	79.3
Of which all or some:		
have general or specific functions other than ERs	18	62.1
Of which:		
all have professional qualifications	7	24.1
some have professional qualifications	18	62.1
none have professional qualifications	4	13.8
Of which:		
all have supporting staff	24	82.7
some have supporting staff	2	6.9
none have supporting staff	3	10.4

3.08c Subsidiary companies, businesses or divisions of multi-establishment companies

	Multi-establishment companies	
	Number	Per cent
Divisions in which no board or management committee has specific responsibility for employee relations	38	43.2
Responsibility for ERs, as and when required, for all or some boards taken by:		
chairman	7	18.4
MD or chief executive	20	52.6
other board member	8	21.0
no response	3	8.0
In which boards employ senior ER executives or managers:		
all divisions	6	15.8
some divisions	6	15.8
no divisions	26	68.4
In which ER executives or managers have supporting staff	12	100.0

3.09a Establishments of multi-establishment companies and divisions

	Multi-establishment companies		Divisions of multis	
	Number	Per cent	Number	Per cent
Companies in which general responsibility for ERs at establishment level is taken by:				
the most senior line manager:				
some	11	10.8	0	0.0
most	7	6.9	4	13.8
all	60	58.8	17	58.6
none	4	3.9	1	3.4
a specialist ER manager:				
some	10	9.8	1	3.4
most	6	5.9	1	3.4
all	10	9.8	4	13.8
none	29	28.4	4	13.8
another manager:				
some	2	2.0	0	0.0
most	0	0.0	0	0.0
all	5	4.9	0	0.0
none	1	1.0	1	3.4
All or most responsible to:				
a main board director	40	39.2	5	17.2
main board ER director	3	2.9	1	3.4
divisional board director	28	27.5	12	41.4
divisional board ER director	3	2.9	3	10.3
other	13	12.7	3	10.3
All or most having day-to-day responsibility for ER:				
most senior line manager	62	60.8	19	65.5
specialist ER manager	21	20.6	6	20.7
other	5	4.9	0	0.0

3.09b Staffing of employee relations – main board and subsidiary boards – companies employing over 1,000 multi-establishment companies

Number of employees	Number of companies	Full-time				Part-time			No directors	Number of full-time and part-time directors
		Main board only	Main & subsid. boards	Subsid. board only	Subsid. P/T main boards	Main board only	Main & subsid. boards	Subsid. board only		
1,001–5,000	24	2	5	2	2	1	5	1	6	18 (0.75)
5,001–10,000	9	1	1	3	1	1	1	0	1	8 (0.84)
10,001–30,000	18	4	4	3	0	1	2	1	3	15 (0.83)
Over 30,000	11	5	1	1	0	3	1	0	0	11 (1.00)
	62	12	11	9	3	6	9	2	10	52 (0.84)

( ) Average number of full- and part-time directors responsible in each size group.

3.09c Staffing of employee relations – allocation of employee relations responsibility at establishments. Multi-establishment companies

Number of employees	Number of companies	Main and subsid. boards			Employee relations responsibility at establishments					
					General			Day-to-day		
		F/T	P/T	Total	Senior line manager	Specialist ER manager	none	Senior line manager	Specialist ER manager	none
1,001–5,000	24	11	7	18	12	5	1	11	6	1
5,001–10,000	9	6	2	8	4	3	1	3	4	1
10,001–30,000	18	11	4	15	10	5	0	8	6	1
Over 30,000	11	7	4	11	7	3	1	3	7	1
	62	35	17	52	33	16	3	25	23	4

3.09d Staffing of employee relations – allocation of employee relations responsibility at establishments. Multi-establishment companies

	Number of companies	Employee relations responsibility at establishments					
		General			Day-to-day		
		Senior line manager	Specialist ER manager	none	Senior line manager	Specialist ER manager	none
Full-time main board director	26	17	11	0	15	3	0
Senior full-time executive not on main board	23	16	9	1	16	9	1
Part-time main board director	31	25	4	0	22	9	0
No main board director or senior full-time executive	22	19	1	3	19	1	3
	102	77	25	4	72	22	4

Where respondents replied that 'some' establishments followed one practice and 'some' followed another, or where responsibilities appeared to be shared, *both* responsible persons have been counted.

3.09e Staffing of employee relations – main, subsidiary and divisional boards – companies employing over 1,000 multi-establishment companies

Number of employees	Number of companies	Main and subsidiary boards			Divisional boards		Establishments F/T specialists		(b) as percent
		F/T	P/T	Total (a)	All/Some	None	All/Some (b)	None	(a)
1,001–5,000	24	11	7	18	8	10(3)	8	10	44.4
5,001–10,000	9	6	2	8	2	6(1)	4	4	50.0
10,001–30,000	18	11	4	15	11	4(0)	9	6	60.0
Over 30,000	11	7	4	11	9	2(0)	9	2	81.8
	62	35	17	52	30	22(4)	30	22	57.7

( ) Companies with no divisional boards.

3.010 Establishments of multi-establishment companies and divisions

	Multi-establishment companies		Divisions of multis	
	Number	Per cent	Number	Per cent
ER specialists recruited:				
Outside with (without) ER skills				
some	28 (1)	27.5(1.0)	3	10.3
most	8	7.8	4	13.8
all	5	4.9	4	13.8
Upgrade or transfer within ER				
some	1	1.0	5	17.2
most	1	1.0	2	6.9
all	4	3.9	1	3.4
Transfer from other function to ER				
some	27 (5)	26.5(4.9)	1	3.4
most	2	2.0	0	0.0
all	1	1.0	0	0.0
ER specialists with professional qualifications:				
some	27	26.5	4	13.8
most	15	14.7	2	6.9
all	1	1.0	4	13.8
none	3	2.9	1	3.4

4 Boards of companies and employee relations

The background

Very little is known about the operation of boards in this country. Very few duties and responsibilities of directors are explicitly laid down by statute. Public companies are required to have a minimum of two directors but are left free in other respects to constitute their boards as they please. Since there is no statutory obligation to report on such matters our general knowledge of their composition and operation is thus drawn from surveys and studies of companies done on a relatively small scale. From these it has been concluded that board size, beyond 7 or 8 directors, increases only modestly with total numbers employed and that, compared, for example, with the United States, main boards of companies tend to be relatively 'active', i.e. to be made up of a majority of full-time company executives who operate on a level of *deciding* and *establishing* to a greater degree than boards in other countries composed mostly of 'outsiders'. We are also told that UK companies in general have relatively few formal committees, typically only a chairman's committee meeting two or three times a year, a finance committee and an executive or management committee, often not strictly a board committee, consisting exclusively of executive directors (and in some cases senior managers) which meets more frequently and is concerned with operational issues and day-to-day business. We have no information in detail on how board arrangements vary by size of company or, relative to the subject of this survey, how they are set out for employee relations purposes, beyond the fact that committees dealing with employee relations do now exist, at least in a minority of companies.

A major question which remains at issue, despite the acknowledged executive nature of board membership, is the extent to which boards initiate their own activity as distinct from ratifying or approving matters formulated elsewhere. A more serious claim is that many, if not most, board directors see themselves as entirely detached from 'people', regarding workers simply as a cost to be minimised and thinking of 'non-contact' or involvement as a positive advantage in the avoidance of a possibly distasteful responsibility or as a strategy for the concealment of underlying intentions. The present chapter throws light on the frequency with which boards discuss employee relations, the subjects of their discussions, with some reflections on their basic role in the area.

Single establishment companies

One hundred and fifty-two of the 156 single establishment companies included in the survey gave information about their active board directors, noting a total of 551, an average of 4 directors to each board, but with numbers ranging from one director to 9 or more (4.1). As noted earlier, six of the companies had a personnel director, four of whom were recorded as having primary responsibility for employee relations.[1] This formed a small proportion of the 98 companies (63 per cent of the total), which had a board member with recognised responsibility for that function, the bulk of these being chairmen or managing directors (59 per cent) or works or production directors (25 per cent) for the most part (79 per cent) spending one quarter or less of their time in that capacity.

Boards of single establishment companies appear to regard employee relations as a somewhat undifferentiated matter to be discussed as and when particular questions claim their attention. Two-thirds of the companies reported that they discussed such matters only 'when necessary'. A few (6.4 per cent) claimed that they never dealt with the subject on the board at all (4.3). A significant minority (17 per cent, with no particular differentiation as to size) reported discussion at 'most meetings' of the board and a small minority (8 per cent) 'at every meeting'. These 'most' and 'every' companies were only marginally more unionised than average for all the single establishment companies in the survey. Ten of them also received regular written reports on employee relations, but in most companies reporting was reported as being by word-of-mouth.

1 See Table 3.2a.

The main board is not, however, the only forum for consideration of employee relations. Two-thirds of the companies had an executive committee for general management purposes. Twenty per cent of these discussed employee relations matters 'always' and 78 per cent 'sometimes'. In addition 92 (or 59 per cent of all companies) had an employee relations committee which met regularly (one in three) or occasionally (two in three) (4.4). Adding these together, companies appeared to be almost 80 per cent covered by 'directors' forums' in which employee relations questions could be raised and discussed, albeit in a somewhat undocumented way.

What is discussed in these forums? Most likely, it seems, matters relating to pay, to methods of getting over information and how to deploy manpower (4.5). In a minority of companies (11 per cent) which make use of *ad hoc* or standing committees on employee relations issues, much the same priorities prevail (4.6). The directors of such companies appear to pay relatively little attention to legislation on labour matters or to issued codes of practice. Overall, such matters have less than an even chance of being discussed by the board (43 per cent of cases; 4.7), though some are more likely to be discussed than others. The main factors in making such a decision may, judging from their content, be closely related to whether an enactment or regulation, in principle or practice involves *cost*, whether it is likely to lead to *concessions to or reactions from trade unions*, to *inspection* or, in a general sense, whether it is likely to affect the company in any substantial way. Measured by these criteria, the Health and Safety at Work Act rated high on all counts and was discussed by 80 per cent of boards. Unfair dismissal, equal pay and the Social Security Pensions Act followed (about 55 per cent), and then matters almost exclusively relating to trade unions — facilities, recognition and the closed shop (35 per cent: more than 40 per cent recognised no trade union). Finally, at the low end of the scale of attention, maternity pay, observation of general terms and conditions and race relations (under 30 per cent) and the Patents Act (under 20 per cent). Verbal reports formed the largest basis for discussion.

Establishments of multi-establishment companies

The pattern of behaviour of boards or management committees of establishments of multis followed with remarkable closeness those of single establishment companies, though with somewhat higher percentages in all cases. Their boards or management committees were a little larger (4.1); they had a higher proportion of personnel directors (4.2); they discussed employee relations a little more frequently and they had a somewhat higher incidence of board executive committees and employee relations committees, which also tended to meet more regularly (4.4). Subjects of board discussion were much the same as in single establishment companies, though with some upgrading of industrial disputes (which were more frequent), management training and redundancy (4.5). In general, more boards had discussed legislation (4.7). Health and safety still topped the bill, but items involving trade unions had a higher priority, these companies being more likely to be unionised.

Being associated as part of a multi-establishment company apparently makes little difference to board or management committee organisation or behaviour compared with 'independent' companies of similar size and type. This seems to confirm the observation made in Chapter 3 that the headquarters of such companies have tended to move with caution in seeking to alter the style of employee relations management in their constituents, though encouraging greater 'professionalism' where this has seemed necessary.

Multi-establishment companies and divisions of multis

Do main boards of multi-establishment companies handle employee relations matters differently from single establishment companies? Table 4a, which compares the regularity with which boards in all four kinds of company situation discuss employees, and Table 4b, which takes a similar overall view of the use of written reports, suggests that although differences do exist, these are relatively small in some respects. Rather *less* than two-thirds (compared with rather *more* than two-thirds in the case of single establishment companies) reported that they discussed employee relations only 'when necessary' and only a negligible number that they were never discussed at all. Conversely almost 35 per cent said that they discussed the subject at 'every meeting' or at 'most meetings' of the board, compared with 26 per cent of single establishment companies. A greater difference was reported where the use of formal written reports are concerned, under 7 per cent of singles noting this practice, compared with a total of 31 per cent for headquarters of multis, which also used written reports almost twice as often.

How is this data to be interpreted? It may readily be supposed that both regular discussion of employee relations and the use of documents and reports are related to the presence of full-time specialists. This is so, at least to some extent (4.02). Where there are full-time directors on main boards employee relations are discussed most regularly and written and special reports are most frequently employed; where no

Table 4a Regularity with which boards or management committees discuss employee relations

Interval	Multi-establishment company		Division of multi		Establishment of multi		Single establishment company	
	No.	%	No.	%	No.	%	No.	%
Every meeting	21	19.1	5	19.2	4	7.5	12	7.9
Most meetings	17	15.5	5	19.2	13	24.5	27	17.9
When necessary	70	63.6	15	57.7	35	66.0	102	67.5
All intervals	108	98.2	25	96.1	52	98.0	141	93.3
Never	2	1.8	1	3.9	1	2.0	10	6.7
All companies	110	100.0	26	100.0	53	100.0	151	100.0

Table 4b Boards or management committees receiving formal written reports at regular intervals or on particular subjects or incidents

	No.	%	No.	%	No.	%	No.	%
Every meeting	16	14.5	3	11.5	4	7.5	10	6.7
Most meetings	18	16.4	1	3.9	0	0.0	0	0.0
On particular subjects or incidents	48	43.6	6	23.1	20	37.7	35	23.2

main board or senior executive is responsible there is a 70 per cent chance that employee relations will only be discussed when problems arise and very little chance that written papers will be produced. But there are evidently large companies in which the main board rarely discusses employee relations, and then only on an *ad hoc* basis, some of these with full-time or part-time employee relations directors.

As in the case of single establishment companies discussion on executive management and employee relations committees are evidently thought of as taking the place of such main board activity. This appears to be the case in some of the largest and best staffed companies in the survey. Nothing is known about *other* questions of strategic or tactical issues which main boards may be supposed to discuss and whether these too are similarly treated. Where employee relations are concerned the conclusion seems to be inescapable that even where these are carefully monitored and catered for, main boards are often content to endorse decisions made elsewhere and only become directly involved where the situation is judged to have become serious enough to merit such attention.

These matters are not, it seems from Table 4c, different in many respects from those discussed by boards at establishment and divisional levels. Pay awards top the list at all levels; communications and consultation, by which it may be supposed that boards discuss the how and when of passing on information, are high on the list. Plainly, boards deal with events and incidents rather than seeking to set parameters as such. Manpower planning, markets and their labour effects come near the bottom of the table; main boards of multis pay greater attention to disputes and redundancies than they do to overall consideration of the labour scene. Employee relations committees appear to do much the same. The model which companies apply seems predominantly to be one of 'action and response' so far as this can be judged from the present information available. A closer examination of the detailed working of boards would be necessary to demonstrate whether such a judgement would ultimately be justified.

Where legislation is concerned, main boards of multis tend more towards receiving written reports and have been more inclined to discuss such matters than boards of single establishment companies (4.07). They have also, it seems, been inclined to discuss legislation or codes relating to matters of principle rather than matters of practice alone.

Subject to more detailed investigation than the present inquiry affords, the general impression remains that it would not be unreasonable to support the view that main boards of multi-establishments tend to distance themselves from employee relations and that, except where legislation is concerned, they tend, like single

Table 4c Subjects most likely to be discussed by boards and employee relations committees

Multi-establishment companies				Divisions of multis				Individual establishment multi		Single establishment	
Main board		Employee relations committee		Divisional board		Employee relations committee		Board or management committee		Board or management committee	
Subject	%	Subject	%	Subject	%	Subject	%	Subject	%	Subject	%
Company pay awards	66.7	Company pay awards	78.3	Company pay awards	62.1	Company pay awards	75.0	Company pay awards	63.0	Company pay awards	51.3
Industrial disputes	55.9	Communica-tion & cons.	73.9	Industrial disputes	} 37.9	Manpower planning	} 50.0	Pay systems	40.7	Pay systems	38.5
Communica-tion & cons.	30.4	Pay systems	43.5	Manpower planning	} 37.9	Pay systems	} 50.0	Communica-tion & cons.	35.2	Communica-tion & cons.	28.8
Pay systems	} 27.5	Industrial disputes	39.1	Redundancy	27.6	Discipline	} 50.0	Industrial disputes	} 29.6	Manpower planning	26.3
Redundancy	} 27.5	Management training	21.7	Communica-tion & cons.	24.1	Markets on employment	} 25.0	Markets on employment	} 29.6	Discipline	23.1
Investment on employment	} 27.5	Redundancy	17.4	Pay systems	20.7	Communica-tion & cons.	} 25.0	Manpower planning	} 27.8	Investment on employment	17.9
Manpower planning	25.5	Manpower planning	13.0	Management training	13.8	Redundancy	} 25.0	Investment on employment	} 27.8	Markets on employment	15.4
Management training	14.7	Discipline	} 8.7	Markets on employment	10.3			Management training	} 20.4	Industrial disputes	12.8
Legal cases	8.8	Investment on employment	} 8.7	Investment on employment	6.9			Redundancy	} 20.4	Management training	10.5
Markets on employment	5.9	Markets on employment	} 8.7	Discipline	3.4			Discipline	18.5	Redundancy	6.4
Discipline	3.9	Legal cases	4.3	Legal cases				Legal cases	5.6	Legal cases	1.9

104

establishment company boards, to respond to situations as they arise or when these are drawn to their attention.

Summary

1 Boards of companies whether single or multi-establishment, are inclined to discuss employee relations only when necessary though there is, in larger and more complex multi-establishment situations a tendency to make such consideration a more regular feature of board practice.
2 Discussion tends to be 'undocumented' at board level, though it may be that a more systematic approach, both in the frequency of consideration of employee relations, and in the supply of papers for consideration, develops where there are 'directors' forums' and especially where there are *ad hoc* or standing committees dealing with employee relations matters.
3 The presence of full-time employee relations directors on main boards tends to make consideration of employee relations more regular and written documentation more likely. The effect of having senior executive employee relations managers or directors with no responsible director on the main board is to discourage regular discussion of employee relations and regular reports but to encourage the use of special reports.
4 Boards of different kinds and sizes appear to have similar priorities in the subjects which they are likely to discuss; boards of multi-establishment companies are not noticeably more likely than others to give preference to planned approaches to manpower issues.
5 The model of behaviour adopted by company boards of all kinds tends to combine an attitude of 'action and response' with a certain 'distancing' from events except where these appear to be related, in the shorter or longer run, to what are considered to be the financial or tactical interests of the company.

References

Booz, Allen and Hamilton, *The Responsibilities and Contribution of Non-executive Directors on the Boards of Companies,* a study for the Institute of Directors, October 1979.
British Institute of Management, *Boards of Directors in Small/medium sized Private Companies,* A Survey of the composition of Boards of Directors in 289 private companies, Information Summary 149, 1970.

British Institute of Management, *The Board of Directors,* A Survey of its structure, composition and role, Management Survey Report No. 10, 1972.

Brooks, Christopher, *Boards of Directors in British Industry*, Department of Employment Research Paper No. 7, August 1979.

Conference Board Inc., Chapter 5, 'United Kingdom' in *Boards of Directors,* Perspective and Practices in Nine Countries, Report No. 728, 1977.

Gordon, R.A., *Business Leadership in Large Corporations,* The Brookings Institution, 1948.

Knight, Ian B., Chapter 3 in *Company Organisation and Worker Participation,* Office of Population Censuses and Surveys, SS 1082, HMSO 1979.

Lindsay, G. *Boards of Directors Study, 1981,* Korn/Ferry International, 1981.

Prentice, D.D., 'A Company and its Employees: The Companies Act 1980', *Industrial Law Journal,* Vol. 10, No. 1, March 1981.

Tricker, Robert, *The Independent Director in the British Company,* Korn/Ferry International, 1979.

Winkler, J.T., 'The Ghost at the Bargaining Table', *British Journal of Industrial Relations,* Vol. XII, No. 2, July 1974.

Tabulations

Boards of companies and employee relations

4.1 Number of active directors

	Single establishment company		Individual establishment multi	
	Number	Per cent	Number	Per cent
1 only	9	5.9	2	4.0
2	36	23.7	4	8.0
3	36	23.7	6	12.0
4	34	22.4	11	22.0
5	17	11.2	8	16.0
6	9	5.9	4	8.0
7	5	3.3	8	16.0
8	4	2.6	3	6.0
9 and more	2	1.3	4	8.0
	152	100.0	50	100.0
Total number of directors noted	551		256	
Average number of directors per company	4		5	

4.2 Principal functions of active directors

	Single establishment company		Individual establishment multi	
	Number	Per cent	Number	Per cent
Chairman	56	35.9	24	44.4
Chairman/MD	34	21.8	10	18.5
Managing director	96	61.5	32	59.3
Joint/deputy MD	41	26.3	16	29.6
Production/works D.	108	69.2	26	48.1
Marketing/sales D.	92	58.9	26	48.1
Personnel	6	3.8	10	18.5
Finance	43	27.6	24	44.4
Technical	23	14.7	22	40.7
Company secretary	18	11.5	5	9.3
Administrative	6	3.8	5	9.3
Non-executive director	3	1.9	8	14.8
Other	21	13.5	41	75.9
	547*		249*	

*A few companies did not specify the role of each director.

4.3 Regularity with which board or management committee discusses employee relations

Interval	Single establishment company		Individual establishment multi	
	Number	Per cent	Number	Per cent
Every meeting	12 (10)	7.7 (6.4)	4 (4)	7.3 (7.3)
Most meetings	27	17.3	13	24.1
When necessary	102	65.4	35	63.0
All intervals	141 *(35)	90.4 *(24.8)	51 *(20)	94.4*(39.2)
Never	10	6.4	1	1.9
No response	5	3.2	2	3.7
	156	100.0	54	100.0

( ) Establishments at which formal written reports are presented at every meeting or quarterly, annually or at other regular intervals.

*( ) Establishments at which special written reports are presented on particular subjects or incidents.

4.4 Executive and employee relations committees of boards

Companies with	Single establishment company		Individual establishment multi	
	Number	Per cent	Number	Per cent
Executive committees for general management purposes	106	66.7	38	70.4
Of which chaired by:				
chairman or MD	79	85.9	32	84.2
other director	25	14.1	6	15.8
Discusses employee relations:				
always	21	19.8	7	18.4
sometimes	83	78.3	30	78.9
never	2	1.9	1	2.6
	106	100.0	38	100.0
Employee relations committee	92	59.0	35	64.8
Which meets:				
regularly	32	34.8	22	62.8
occasionally	60	65.2	13	37.2
	92	100.0	35	100.0
Chaired by:				
chairman/MD	75	81.5	26	74.3
production director	3	3.3	2	5.7
personnel director	1	1.1	2	5.7
other director	13	14.1	5	14.3
	92	100.0	35	100.0
Advisers attend:				
always	2	2.2	0	0.0
sometimes	19	20.6	9	25.7
never	71	77.2	26	74.3
	92	100.0	35	100.0

4.5 Subjects most and least likely to be discussed by boards or employee relations committees

Subject	Single establishment company		Individual establishment multi	
	Most likely	Least likely	Most likely	Least likely
	Per cent		Per cent	
Company pay awards	51.3	2.6	63.0	3.7
Pay systems and structures	38.5	9.6	40.7	9.3
Communication and consultation	28.8	6.4	35.2	5.6
Manpower planning	26.3	6.4	27.8	11.1
Discipline	23.1	15.4	18.5	27.8
Effects of investment on employment	17.9	23.7	20.4	27.8
Effects of markets on employment	15.4	21.2	29.6	27.8
Industrial disputes	12.8	41.0	29.6	40.7
Management training	10.5	12.8	20.4	13.0
Redundancy	6.4	39.1	20.4	37.0
Legal cases affecting company	1.9	39.1	5.6	55.6

4.6 Ad hoc committees or standing committees on particular employee relations issues

	Single establishment company		Individual establishment multi	
	Number	Per cent	Number	Per cent
Use ad hoc or standing committees	17	10.9	10	18.5
On issues:				
job evaluation	3	17.6	2	20.0
productivity schemes	2	11.8	1	10.0
incentive schemes	3	17.6	1	10.0
grading	2	11.8	0	0.0
special projects/ unexpected issues	3	17.6	0	0.0
flexi-time	2	11.8	0	0.0
consultation/ communication	2	11.8	2	20.0
revision of agreements/ preparation of company policies	2	11.8	0	0.0
wage reviews	1	5.9	3	30.0
health and safety	1	5.9	0	0.0
suggestions scheme	1	5.9	0	0.0
discipline	0	0.0	1	10.0
organisation and method	0	0.0	1	10.0
sick pay	0	0.0	1	10.0
holidays	0	0.0	1	10.0
shorter working week	0	0.0	1	10.0
miscellaneous	4	23.5	4	40.0

4.7 Company board discussion of legislative provisions

Single establishment companies

	Discussed by board before statutory implementation			Not discussed at any time by board
	Written report	Verbal report only	Verbal and written report	
			per cent N = 156	
Health and Safety Act	12.2	46.8	17.3	19.2
Unfair Dismissal	1.9	46.8	3.8	42.9
Equal Pay	3.2	39.1	8.3	44.9
Soc. Security Pensions Act	7.1	28.2	14.1	46.2
Disclosure of Information	0.6	35.3	3.2	56.4
Trade Union Recognition	2.6	28.2	4.5	60.3
Facilities for TUs	0.6	29.5	3.8	61.5
Union M'ship Agreements	1.3	23.1	4.5	66.7
Maternity Pay	0.6	23.7	2.6	68.6
Schedule 11 EP Act	0.6	21.2	4.5	69.2
Race Relations Act	0.0	20.5	3.8	71.2
Patents Act	0.6	12.8	1.3	80.8
(Average)	(2.4)	(29.6)	(6.0)	(57.3)

Individual establishment companies

Health and Safety Act	14.8	22.2	37.0	16.7
Soc. Security Pensions Act	5.6	24.1	31.5	29.6
Unfair Dismissal	3.7	33.3	18.5	35.2
Disclosure of Information	3.7	22.2	25.9	38.9
Equal Pay	1.9	27.8	18.5	42.6
Union M'ship Agreements	0.0	33.3	9.3	48.1
Facilities for TUs	0.0	31.5	9.3	50.0
Schedule 11 EP Act	0.0	33.3	7.4	50.0
Trade Union Recognition	3.7	27.8	7.4	51.9
Maternity Pay	1.9	24.1	11.1	53.7
Race Relations Act	0.0	25.9	1.9	63.0
Patents Act	1.9	14.8	5.6	68.5
(Average)	(3.2)	(26.7)	(15.3)	(45.7)

4.01 Regularity with which main boards or management committees or divisional boards or management committees discuss employee relations

Interval	Multi-establishment company		Division of multi	
	Number	Per cent	Number	Per cent
			Parent company	
Every meeting	19 (15)	18.6 (14.7)	2 (1)	6.9 (3.4)
Most meetings	16 (16)	15.7 (15.7)	1 (2)	3.4 (6.9)
When necessary	62	60.8	8	27.6
All intervals	97 (42)*	95.1 (43.3)*	11 (6)*	37.9 (20.7)*
Never	2	2.0	2	6.9
No response	3	2.4	7	24.2
Don't know			9	31.0
	102	100.0	29	100.0
			Divisional boards	
Every meeting	–	–	5 (3)	17.2 (10.3)
Most meetings	–	–	5 (1)	17.2 (3.4)
When necessary	–	–	15	51.7
All intervals			25 (9)*	86.2 (31.0)*
Never			1	3.4
No response			3	10.4
			29	100.0

( )   Companies or divisions in which formal written reports are presented at every meeting, quarterly, annually or at other intervals.

( ) *   Companies or divisions in which special reports are presented on particular subjects or incidents.

4.02 Regularity with which main board discusses employee relations: multi-establishment companies and issues formal and special written reports.
(Percentages)

Multi-establishment companies with	No.	Intervals			Issues	
		Every meeting	Most meetings	When necessary	Written reports	Special reports
		Per cent			Per cent	
Full-time employee relations director on main board	26	35	27	35	38	81
Part-time employee relations director on main board	31	19	7	74	32	32
Senior executive director or manager but no main board director	23	13	17	62 (4)	13	39
No main board or senior executive responsible for employee relations	22	9	14	69 (4)	0	4
	102	21	17	61 (1)	22	41

( ) = never

115

4.03 Employee relations committees of company main boards or divisional boards

	Multi-establishment company		Division of	
	Number	Per cent	Number	Per cent
Companies or divisions with employee relations committees	23	22.5	4	13.8
Which meet:				
weekly	2	8.7	0	0.0
fortnightly	0	0.0	1	25.0
monthly	9	39.1	2	50.0
quarterly	5	21.7	0	0.0
other	7	30.5	1	25.0
	23	100.0	4	100.0

4.04 Employee relations committees of company main boards with and without directors responsible for employee relations

Multi-establishment companies with	Employee relations committees		All companies
	Number	Per cent	
Full-time employee relations directors on main boards	12	46.1	26
Part-time employee relations directors on main boards	6	19.4	31
Senior executive director or manager, but no main board director	5	21.7	23
No main board director or senior executive responsible for employee relations	0	0.0	22
	23	22.5	102

4.05 Subjects most and least likely to be discussed by main and divisional boards and employee relations committees

Subject	Multi-establishment company		Division of multi	
	Most likely	Least likely	Most likely	Least likely
	Per cent		Per cent	
Company pay awards	66.7 (78.3)	2.0 (0.0)	62.1 (75.0)	0.0 (0.0)
Pay systems and structures	27.5 (43.5)	19.6 (21.7)	20.7 (50.0)	17.2 (25.0)
Communication and consultation	30.4 (73.9)	9.8 (4.3)	24.1 (25.0)	17.2 (0.0)
Manpower planning	25.5 (13.0)	15.7 (21.7)	37.9 (50.0)	10.3 (25.0)
Discipline	3.9 (8.7)	62.7 (0.0)	3.4 (50.0)	51.7 (0.0)
Effects of investment on employment	27.5 (8.7)	12.7 (39.1)	6.9 (0.0)	24.1 (25.0)
Effects of markets on employment	5.9 (8.7)	40.2 (52.2)	10.3 (25.0)	31.0 (75.0)
Industrial disputes	55.9 (39.1)	18.6 (17.4)	37.9 (0.0)	10.3 (75.0)
Management training	14.7 (21.7)	23.5 (21.7)	13.8 (0.0)	10.3 (0.0)
Redundancy	27.5 (17.4)	22.5 (21.7)	27.6 (25.0)	17.2 (50.0)
Legal cases affecting company	8.8 (4.3)	49.0 (47.8)	3.4 (0.0)	48.3 (25.0)
N =	102 (23)	102 (23)	29 (4)	29 (4)

( ) Designates employee relations committees.

4.06 Ad hoc or standing committees of main or divisional boards on particular employee relations issues

	Multi-establishment companies		Divisions of multis	
	Number	Per cent	Number	Per cent
Use ad hoc or standing committees	23	22.5	5	17.2
on issues:				
pay	8	34.8	3	60.0
fringe benefits	3	13.0	0	0.0
pensions	2	8.7	1	20.0
incentive schemes	0	0.0	1	20.0
share option scheme	2	8.7	0	0.0
reduced working week	2	8.7	0	0.0
staff incentive scheme	1	4.3	0	0.0
conditions	1	4.3	0	0.0
EPA–or similar	3	13.0	0	0.0
industrial democracy	4	17.4	0	0.0
director's remuneration	2	8.7	0	0.0
staff grading structure	1	4.3	1	20.0
job evaluation	1	4.3	1	20.0
communications	1	4.3	1	20.0
management development	3	13.0	0	0.0
health and safety	2	8.7	0	0.0
disclosure to TU	1	4.3	0	0.0
miscellaneous	11	47.8	3	30.0

4.07 Company main boards. Discussion of legislative provisions

Multi-establishment company

	Discussed by board before statutory implementation			Not discussed at any time by board
	Written report	Verbal report only	Verbal and written report	
	Per cent N = 156			
Health and Safety Act	4.9	20.6	25.5	24.5
Unfair Dismissal	4.9	24.5	13.7	31.4
Equal Pay	4.9	23.5	17.6	28.4
Soc. Security Pensions Act	9.8	8.8	27.5	28.4
Disclosure of Information	8.8	19.6	19.6	27.5
Trade Union Recognition	5.9	14.7	21.6	32.4
Facilities for TUs.	4.9	13.7	13.7	42.2
Union M'ship Agreements	2.0	16.7	19.6	36.3
Maternity Pay	2.0	16.7	9.8	46.1
Schedule 11 EP Act	2.9	10.8	14.7	46.1
Race Relations Act	1.0	11.8	12.7	48.0
Patents Act	2.0	10.8	12.7	49.0
Sex Discrimination	2.9	13.7	13.7	44.1
	4.2	15.8	17.1	37.3

5 Participation, consultation and communication

Background

The present situation on participation, consultation and communication in companies in British industry can be thought of as representing a series of tide marks left over time by attempts in one way or another to involve employees in the conduct of their establishments.

Early nineteenth century essays in participation have left little behind except the names and doctrines of idealistic reformers such as Robert Owen, the Rochdale Pioneers and the Chartists. Later developments based upon creeds more specifically Marxist or socialist in character rose and fell towards the end of the century and were revived in the syndicalist and Guild Socialist phase which preceded and followed the first world war. The post-war depressions and the prolonged slump in the early 1930s effectively removed such aspirations from the social/industrial scene and, although many supporters of industrial democracy remained to be found in the labour movement, it was not wholly revived as a popular issue until the issue by the Labour Party of a working party report on *Industrial Democracy* in 1967. In the climate of that time, stimulated by a draft Fifth Directive for the European Economic Community issued in 1972 recommending universal works councils and participation on the German/Dutch models, the participation issue became a live political question which both the Heath and Wilson governments attempted to tackle, the latter on lines recommended by the Bullock Committee of Inquiry on Industrial Democracy which reported in January 1977.

The efforts of both Conservative and Labour governments and of the EEC proved abortive, but not without bringing about a lively debate and a revival of interest in participative methods. Three of these can be distinguished—a revival of joint consultation, attention to disclosure of information and developments in communications.

Joint consultation, sometimes wrongly regarded as originating in the reports of the Whitley Committee of 1916—1918, was a product of the second world war, having its origins in the joint production consultative and advisory committees agreed between the unions and the engineering employers in 1942. After the war such committees fell away. They were sometimes associated with works councils which had survived the depression, usually as non-union bodies, and found it difficult to withstand the development of collective bargaining as a more effective way, from a trade union point of view at least, of obtaining a say in company affairs. In the 1970s they began to revive as employers sought to deepen their relationships with employees in a non-negotiating framework as far as this was possible.

At about the same time the Industrial Relations Act 1971 reflected in its terms the belief of many that much could be gained from urging upon employers and making statutory provision for disclosure of company information. This led to a remarkable growth in versions of company reports designed for employee use (and commonly known as 'employee reports'), and attempts to extend the information made available by employers to trade unions for collective bargaining. While the latter seems to have reached its peak before the end of the Callaghan government in 1979, employee reporting has continued, together with a vogue for briefing groups designed to reinforce worker-management co-operation at successively higher levels in companies through orthodox supervisory and executive channels and with a revival of interest in communication techniques and problems generally. Although some companies adopted such refinements after the last war, systematic approaches to communications, which owed much to the 'human relations' school developed by the American sociologist Elton Mayo from the 1920s onwards, had only limited publicity until the middle 1950s. Since that time they have attracted particular attention, especially in the 1970s.

The survey data gives some indication of the state of these developments in the companies which took part at the beginning of 1980 and of the attention which, at the appropriate time some two or three years earlier, they had paid to the Bullock Report.

Consultation has, at least since the 1960s, been identified under two heads, *formal* and *informal*. Formal consultation is that which takes place between managements and representatives of employees, usually but not invariably at works level, within an established committee

Table 5A Company style in employee participation

	Multi-establishment company		Division of multi		Establishment of multi		Single establishment company	
	Today Per cent	In the past Per cent	Today Per cent	In the past Per cent	Today Per cent	In the past Per cent	Today Per cent	In the past Per cent
Paternalistic	26.4	71.5	27.5	68.9	22.2	38.9	48.7	64.1
Autocratic	6.9	48.1	13.8	55.2	1.9	33.3	6.4	31.4
Participative	69.6	22.6	72.4	24.1	74.1	42.6	74.4	43.6
Negotiating	48.1	26.5	44.8	31.0	35.2	22.2	41.1	32.7
Consultative	64.7	30.4	79.3	27.6	63.0	35.2	68.6	43.6

Table 5B Headquarters, divisions and establishments with works councils and committees, with or without trade union membership, and joint consultative committees

Number of councils, committees or JPCs	HQ of multi-establishment company		Division of multi		Establishment of multi		Single establishment company	
	Number	Per cent	Number	Per cent	Number	Per cent	Number	Per cent
with:								
one only	40	39.2	13	44.8	24	44.4	59	37.8
two	8	7.8	6	20.7	9	16.7	18	11.5
three	7	6.9	1	3.5	2	3.7	11	7.1
No committee	47	46.1	9	31.0	19	35.2	68	43.6
	102	100.0	29	100.0	54	100.0	156	100.0

system, involving regular membership and regular minuted meetings; informal consultation is commonly regarded as that which takes place on a day-to-day basis between supervision and employees jointly and severally in their departments and through which the views of the shop floor are sought on changes being made or about to be made, or on the method to be used in doing various jobs. Informal consultation has as one of its objects the avoidance of problems which may arise through unheralded modifications of working arrangements and conditions. It is sometimes, for this reason, equated with 'prior consultation'. Where trade unions are involved it may be concerned both to avoid and to anticipate collective bargaining. A similar situation may also be found in joint consultation for, although the original consultative committees set up under the 1942 agreement made no special provision for shop stewards to be involved, this has frequently turned out to be the case. Terminology is also a source of complication in this area. Around the end of the first world war joint bodies were commonly known as 'works councils' or 'works committees'. Between the wars these developed a reputation as non-union bodies and were often shunned by organised workers. Since that time some more recently created committees have retained that character, but others have not, while in other cases the term 'joint consultative committee' has been preferred.

Single establishment companies

Single establishment companies without any doubt regard themselves as somewhat less paternalistic and dramatically less autocratic than they were in the past; they also believe themselves to be substantially more participative and consultative (Table 5A). More than 85 per cent claim to practise informal consultation (5.5) and 56 per cent to have consultative committees under one title or another, almost 19 per cent having more than one committee (Table 5B). We have no information on the date of foundation of these committees but the figure is sufficiently high to make it likely that some are of comparatively recent origin. Briefing groups, for the most part a creation of the 1970s are less popular—15 per cent of companies—but some are claimed to have been in existence from the 1950s (5.5).

For one reason or another, or in one form or another, boards of single-establishment companies regarded communication and consultation as an item of some priority, placing this third after pay and pay systems (5.2). This had led almost 22 per cent of them into publishing employee reports and more than half into organising face-to-face meetings with employees to present financial information, although not usually on a regular basis (5.6). Company journals or newspapers were comparatively rare—11.5 per cent of companies—and usually quarterly where they existed (5.7). Almost two-thirds claimed to be liberal in providing information to employees, doing this freely on request, or whether requested or not, although a number were cautious about disclosing information that was too detailed and about revealing individual salaries (5.1). Very few appeared to have clarified in any formal sense the practical issues in disclosing information for collective bargaining purposes (5.3a and b). Where trade unions were not recognised (i.e. in two-fifths of the companies) the most favoured ways of obtaining the views of employees was by day-to-day contact and an 'open door' policy. Relatively few such companies had formal consultative machinery and only two had representative staff associations, although about one in three claimed to arrange periodic discussions with employees; rather more than one-half relied on normal supervisory channels for the purpose (5.4).

With an eye on the future, companies were asked whether they had a policy on participation beyond the use of consultation, i.e. whether they were practising or proposing to practise trade union or other representation on boards or in relation to certain management functions in financial, marketing or production (5.8). Of the small number of companies which replied that they were concerned with board involvement, one reported that an employee had been appointed as a director. The rest gave a variety of answers short of such membership—being present at certain committees, access to the pensions committee or membership of the health and safety committee, or simply explained that since the company was small, senior managers became involved in board business as a matter of convenience. Much more enthusiasm was evinced for the idea that there might be involvement, presumably on an *ad hoc* or more or less informal way, with plant development, product planning, selling and marketing, the first being approved by almost one-third of the companies. If there is to be involvement, the preference seems to be for this to be 'operational' in character and, very probably, an extension of the widely approved device of 'informal consultation'.

Establishments of multis

The *pattern* of consultation and communication practice in establishments of multi-establishment companies was remarkably similar to that in single establishment companies but showed greater apparent commitment to such practices, of whatever kind. Almost two-thirds claimed to have formal committees for consultative purposes, compared with rather more than one-half (Table 5 B); over 90 per cent said that they practised informal consultation, a figure higher by more than 7 per cent (5.5);

briefing groups were more widespread (44 per cent, compared with 15 per cent); company newspapers and employee reporting were more common (5.6 and 5.7); marginally more were liberal in their attitudes to providing information to employees (5.1). The establishments were, of course, on average larger; they were also affected by the policies of parent companies and were more likely to be organised by trade unions. These are among the factors which seem to affect this kind of activity and, as a later chapter shows, increase the degree of *formality* with which employee relations are conducted.

Multi-establishment companies and divisions of multis

It might be expected that from headquarter and divisional levels of multi-establishment companies the greater commitment to consultative and communication systems would be continued. This is generally, but not completely, or entirely consistently, so.

At board level in multi-establishment companies discussion of consultation and communication seems to have ranked about as high as at single establishment companies and at individual establishments (5.02). It appears to have ranked lower at divisions, perhaps because of the need to take account of views expressed from headquarters. At the same time it appears that few divisions had such advice from a higher level, at any rate so far as disclosure of information is concerned (5.04). Both headquarters and divisions reported a shift towards participation and consultation in their management style comparable with that at other levels (Table 5A). Divisions had a somewhat higher percentage of consultative type committees than singles or individual establishments, in that order. There were proportionately fewer recorded at headquarters (Table 5B). Many headquarters staffs were, of course, very small and some associated with divisional or works staff as a whole, making it difficult to see what conclusion, if any, can be drawn from this fact. There is no doubt, however, that multi-establishment companies saw formal consultation as existing very widely in their establishments and that it was the view of at least one-half of them that the practice ought to be encouraged, although divisions showed some disagreement as to whether this was true where their headquarters were concerned (5.010). Briefing groups were, on the information supplied, more used at headquarters and divisions (32.5 and 34.5 per cent respectively) than they were at single establishments (15.4 per cent), but less than at establishments of multis (44.4 per cent). Headquarters of multis were in about four out of ten cases prepared to say that they encouraged them, most of these believing that they worked satisfactorily. Divisions appeared more sceptical of both contentions.

Of the belief among the headquarters of companies that they are in favour of a freer rather than a more restricted flow of information to employees there is no doubt; divisions are again more sceptical (5.01). Employee reports have also become more popular in recent years. Almost 60 per cent of the multi-establishment companies in the survey claimed to issue them. Divisions were less concerned in this development. It is understandable that it would not in all cases be appropriate for them to make such an issue, but they also appeared to see their head-quarters as little more committed than themselves. There was much more accord between the two levels on the use of face-to-face meetings with employees to give financial information (68 and 66 per cent respectively), but this was not high compared with recorded practice at single establishment companies (52.6 per cent) and individuals of multis (68.5 per cent (5.08 and 5.6)). Company journals were issued from head office in 56 per cent of cases and from divisions in 52 per cent, almost all on a monthly or quarterly basis (5.09).

As to the future, 60 per cent of multi-establishment companies recorded that their main boards had discussed the Bullock proposals on worker directors and a further 13 per cent that, even if no discussion had taken place, other action had been taken. Divisions, perhaps because they were in many cases foreign based, noted fewer board discussions, and very few were clear that they had received any instruction or advice on the matter (5.011). Very few appeared to be willing to commit them-selves to a radically changed pattern of employee, or trade union, involvement. In total eight only, consisting of six multis and two divisions spoke of trade union representation on boards or management committees, while ten spoke of non-union involvement.

Where participation beyond existing patterns of consultation was approved, this related to much the same areas as noted in the case of single establishment companies and individual establishments of multis, namely on such issues as plant and factory development and product planning, but even here the enthusiasm for such moves seems to be weaker (5.010). The industrial democracy debate of the 1970s appears to have stimulated some companies to greater effort in doing things which, in many cases, they were already doing in the area of employee participation; others have been stimulated to tread for the first time along well worn paths of worker involvement. Few, if any, appear to have been stimulated to push out the boat into unknown and uncharted waters.

Summary

1 Companies see themselves as having given consultation and communication with their employees some priority in the development of their employee relations; the nearer the workplace, the more feeling there seems to be about such a priority, which has taken a number of forms.

2 Joint consultation, despite predictions of its demise which have been common since the war, appears to be alive and well, both in its formal and informal application.

3 There is a general advocacy of a freer flow of information to employees, although a substantial number of single establishment companies see a 'need to know' or very restricted basis of communication as sufficient and most establishments see subject matter on which limitations ought to be placed.

4 A substantial minority of multi-establishment companies appear to have addressed themselves formally to the application of the disclosure of information for collective bargaining provisions of recent legislation; at division and establishment level, the extent of attention has been much lower.

5 Employee reporting has become common in larger companies, both in written reports and in face-to-face meetings.

6 Company newspapers or journals are also common among larger companies. They are commonly issued monthly or quarterly.

7 Briefing groups have become most common at establishments of multis and are least common among single establishment companies, although a few of this latter type of company claim to have adopted the practice many years ago.

8 Debate about the Bullock Report and other participative happenings of the 1970s brought a good deal of attention at board level but showed little inclination for a radically changed pattern of employee, or trade union, involvement at board or other levels.

References

Brannen, P., Batstone, E., Fatchett, D. and White, P. *The Worker Directors*, Hutchinson, 1976.

British Institute of Management. *Employee Participation: a Management View*, BIM, 1975.

Bullock Report. *Report of the Committee of Inquiry on Industrial Democracy*, Cmnd. 6705, HMSO, January 1977.

Clegg, Chris, W. et al. 'Managers' attitudes towards industrial democracy', *Industrial Relations Journal*, Vol.9, No.3, Autumn 1978.

Commission of the European Communities. 'Employee participation and company structure', *Bulletin of the European Communities*, Supplement 8/75.

Confederation of British Industry. *Evidence to the Bullock Committee of Inquiry*, March 1976.

Engineering Employers' Federation. *Employee Participation*, EEF, November 1974.

Farnham, D. and Pimlott, J. 'Who wants Bullock?' *New Society*, March 3, 1977.

Guest, D. and Fatchett, D. 'Worker Participation: Industrial Control and Performance', Institute of Personnel Management, 1974.

Industrial Democracy, Cmnd. 7231, HMSO, May 1978.

Knight, Ian B. *Company Organisation and Worker Participation*, Office of Population Censuses and Surveys, SS 1082, HMSO, 1979.

Marsden, David. *Industrial Democracy and Industrial Control in West Germany, France and Britain*, Research Paper No.4, Department of Employment, September 1978.

Marsh, A.I. and Hussey, R. *Employee Reporting and Disclosure of Information* (forthcoming).

Trades Union Congress. *Industrial Democracy*, July 1974.

Tabulations

Participation, consultation and communication

5.1 Policy on communication of information to employees

	Single establishment company		Individual establishment multi	
	Number	Per cent	Number	Per cent
'Need-to-know'	21	13.5	6	11.1
Provided on request when useful to company	35	22.4	11	20.4
Provided freely on request	49	31.4	14	25.9
Free flow, whether requested or not	51	32.7	23	42.6
	156	100.0	54	100.0
If free flow, limitations	43	84.3	22	95.6
of which:				
no detailed financial info.	15	34.9	2	9.1
no access individual salaries	10	23.2	6	27.3
company privacy	3	7.0	7	31.8
sources of funding	7	16.3	3	13.6
pricing	4	9.3	4	18.2
other reasons	4	9.3	–	
	43	100.0	22	100.0

5.2 Subjects most and least likely to be discussed by boards or
employee relations committees

Subject	Single establishment company		Individual establishment multi	
	Most likely	Least likely	Most likely	Least likely
	Per cent		Per cent	
Company pay awards	51.3	2.6	63.0	3.7
Pay systems and structures	38.5	9.6	40.7	9.3
Communication and consultation	28.8	6.4	35.2	5.6
Manpower planning	26.3	6.4	27.8	11.1
Discipline	23.1	15.4	18.5	27.8
Effects of investment on employment	17.9	23.7	20.4	27.8
Effects of markets on employment	15.4	21.2	29.6	27.8
Industrial disputes	12.8	41.0	29.6	40.7
Management training	10.5	12.8	20.4	13.0
Redundancy	6.4	39.1	20.4	37.0
Legal cases affecting company	1.9	39.1	5.6	55.6

5.3a Written and unwritten advice to managers on employee relations practice: where trade unions are to any extent recognised

	Single establishment company		Individual establishment multi	
	Number	Per cent	Number	Per cent
Companies recognising	93	59.6	39	78.2
Issuing written advice on further recognition or present recognition	8	8.6	3	7.7
Giving unwritten advice on further recognition or present recognition	26	27.9	10	25.6

	Manual	Non-manual	Manual	Non-manual
		Per cent		
Giving written advice or instruction on:				
facilities for trade unions	19.3	12.9	30.8	23.1
disclosure of information for collective bargaining	4.3	4.3	10.3	7.7
individual and collective grievance handling	53.8	39.8	74.3	66.7
handling of discipline	58.0	41.9	82.0	74.4
implementation of holiday arrangements	61.3	51.6	79.5	76.9
sick pay implementation	38.7	39.8	64.1	64.1
recruitment	20.4	16.1	43.6	41.0
selection	18.3	15.0	33.3	28.0
transfer	15.0	12.9	28.2	30.8

5.3b Written and unwritten advice to managers on employee relations practice: where trade unions are not recognised

	Single establishment company		Individual establishment multi	
	Number	Per cent	Number	Per cent
Companies not recognising	63	40.4	15	21.8
Issuing written advice on attitudes to or action on recognition	2	3.2	0	0.0
Giving unwritten advice on attitudes to or action on recognition	15	23.8	5	33.3

	Manual	Non-manual	Manual	Non-manual
		Per cent		
Giving written advice or instructions on:				
individual and collective grievance handling	15.9	15.9	46.7	46.7
handling of discipline	17.5	17.5	46.7	46.7
implementation of holiday arrangements	39.7	39.7	73.3	73.3
sick pay implementation	30.1	34.9	60.0	53.3
recruitment	7.9	6.3	6.7	13.3
selection	1.6	1.6	0.0	6.7
transfer	1.6	0.0	6.7	6.7

5.4 Method of obtaining the views of employees where no trade
   unions are recognised

	Single establishment company		Individual establishment multi	
	Number	Per cent	Number	Per cent
Companies not recognising	63	40.4	15	21.8
Obtain views of employees through:				
normal super-visory channels	35	55.5	9	60.0
day-to-day contact	49	77.8	11	73.3
open door policy	48	76.2	12	80.0
periodic discussion with employees	23	36.5	9	60.0
works (advisory) council	8	12.7	2	13.3
consultative committees	11	17.5	4	26.7
representative staff association	2	3.8	1	6.7

5.5   Consultation and communication

	Single establishment company		Individual establishment multi	
	Number	Per cent	Number	Per cent
Formal consultation				
works councils or committees of employees	54	34.6	19	35.2
works councils or committees of trade unionists	49	31.4	21	38.9
joint consultative committees	25	16.0	8	14.8
Informal consultation				
management practices	133	85.3	50	92.6
Briefing groups				
used by management	24	15.4	24	44.4
began:				
1979	6	25.0	4	16.8
1978	2	8.3	7	29.2
1977	3	12.5	3	12.5
1971–1976	7	29.2	8	33.3
1965–1970	2	8.3	1	4.2
1960–1964	1	4.2	0	0.0
1955–1959	1	4.2	0	0.0
1950–1954	0	0.0	0	0.0
Before 1950	2	8.3	0	0.0
no response	0	0.0	1	4.2
	24	100.0	24	100.0

5.6 Employee reporting

Companies	Single establishment company		Individual establishment multi	
	Number	Per cent	Number	Per cent
Issuing employee reports	34	21.8	23	42.6
Organising face-to face meetings to give financial information	82	52.6	37	68.5
Of which held:				
regularly	19	23.2	17	45.9
from time to time	63	76.8	20	54.1
		100.0		100.0

5.7 Company journal or newspaper

	Single establishment company		Individual establishment multi	
	Number	Per cent	Number	Per cent
No journal or newspaper	138	88.5	25	46.3
Journal or newspaper	18	11.5	29	53.7
Of which issued:				
weekly	1	0.6	–	–
monthly	2	11.1	–	–
quarterly	12	66.6	–	–
annually	2	11.1	–	–
irregularly	1	0.6	–	–
		100.0		
Of which issued:				
at establishment level			12	41.4
at divisional level			4	13.8
at parent company level			13	44.8
				100.0

5.8 Policy on participation beyond the use of consultation

	Single establishment company		Individual establishment multi	
	Number	Per cent	Number	Per cent
Representation of trade unions on board or management committee	5	3.2	0	0.0
Non-trade union representation on board or management committee	13	8.3	5	9.3
Representation of trade unions or employees in:				
financial planning	11	7.1	5	9.3
marketing policy	15	9.6	7	13.0
selling policy	16	10.3	6	11.1
factory development	50	32.1	13	24.1
product planning	25	16.0	11	20.4
other	17	10.9	8	14.8

5.01 Policy on communication of information to employees

	Multi-establishment company		Division of multi	
	Number	Per cent	Number	Per cent
'Need-to-know'	7	6.9	3	10.3
Provided on request when useful to company	16	15.7	10	34.5
Provided freely on request	26	25.5	5	17.2
Free flow, whether requested or not	51	50.0	10	34.5
No response	2	2.0	1	3.4
	102	100.0	29	100.0
If free flow, limitations	45	44.1	9	31.0
Of which:				
no detailed financial info.	7	15.6	2	22.2
no access individual salaries	10	22.2	3	33.4
company privacy	3	6.7	2	22.2
sources of funding	0	0.0	0	0.0
pricing, orders etc.	6	13.3	1	11.1
company information of use to competitors	11	24.4	–	–
information on market shares	4	8.9	–	–
other reasons	4	8.9	1	11.1

5.02 Subjects most and least likely to be discussed by main and divisional boards and employee relations committees

Subject	Multi-establishment company		Division of multi	
	Most likely	Least likely	Most likely	Least likely
	Per cent		Per cent	
Company pay awards	66.7 (78.3)	2.0 (0.0)	62.1 (75.0)	0.0 (0.0)
Pay systems and structures	27.5 (43.5)	19.6 (21.7)	20.7 (50.0)	17.2 (25.0)
Communication and consultation	30.4 (73.9)	9.8 (4.3)	24.1 (25.0)	17.2 (0.0)
Manpower planning	25.5 (13.0)	15.7 (21.7)	37.9 (50.0)	10.3 (25.0)
Discipline	3.9 (8.7)	62.7 (0.0)	3.4 (50.0)	51.7 (0.0)
Effects of investment on employment	27.5 (8.7)	12.7 (39.1)	6.9 (0.0)	24.1 (25.0)
Effects of markets on employment	5.9 (8.7)	40.2 (52.2)	10.3 (25.0)	31.0 (75.0)
Industrial disputes	55.9 (39.1)	18.6 (17.4)	37.9 (0.0)	10.3 (75.0)
Management training	14.7 (21.7)	23.5 (21.7)	13.8 (0.0)	10.3 (0.0)
Redundancy	27.5 (17.4)	22.5 (21.7)	27.6 (25.0)	17.2 (50.0)
Legal cases affecting company	8.8 (4.3)	49.0 (47.8)	3.4 (0.0)	48.3 (25.0)
N =	102 (23)	102 (23)	29 (4)	29 (4)

(   ) Designates employee relations committees.

5.03 Company main boards: discussion of legislative provisions

	Multi-establishment company			
	Discussed by board before statutory implementation			Not discussed at any time by board
	Written report	Verbal report only	Verbal and written report	
	Per cent N = 156			
Health and Safety Act	4.9	20.6	25.5	24.5
Unfair Dismissal	4.9	24.5	13.7	31.4
Equal Pay	4.9	23.5	17.6	28.4
Social Security Pensions Act	9.8	8.8	27.5	28.4
Disclosure of Information	8.8	19.6	19.6	27.5
Trade Union Recognition	5.9	14.7	21.6	32.4
Facilities for TUs	4.9	13.7	13.7	42.2
Union M'ship Agreements	2.0	16.7	19.6	36.3
Maternity Pay	2.0	16.7	9.8	46.1
Schedule 11 EP Act	2.9	10.8	14.7	46.1
Race Relations Act	1.0	11.8	12.7	48.0
Patents Act	2.0	10.8	12.7	49.0
Sex Discrimination	2.9	13.7	13.7	44.1
	4.2	15.8	17.1	37.3

5.04 Divisions receiving advice or instructions from company head office on the implementation of employee relations legislation

	Advice	Information and advice	Neither
	Per cent N = 29		
Health and Safety Act	13.8	10.3	17.2
Social Security Pensions Act	17.2	6.9	17.2
Unfair Dismissal	13.8	3.4	24.1
Disclosure of Information	3.4	6.9	3.4
Equal Pay	20.7	3.4	17.2
Union M'ship Agreements	3.4	10.3	3.4
Facilities for TUs	10.3	3.4	27.6
Schedule 11 EP Act	6.9	10.3	3.4
Trade Union Recognition	17.2	3.4	20.7
Maternity Pay	6.9	13.8	3.4
Race Relations Act	6.9	6.9	3.4
Patents Act	10.3	10.3	3.4
Sex Discrimination Act	13.8	6.9	17.2
Average	11.1	7.4	12.4

5.05a Written and unwritten advice to managers on employee relations practice from company or divisional head office: where trade unions are to any extent recognised

	Multi-establishment company			Division of multi	
	Number	Per cent		Number	Per cent
Company or division recognising	90	88.2		24	82.8
Issuing written advice on further recognition or present recognition	30	33.3	Parent company	3	12.5
			Division	2	8.3
Giving unwritten advice on further recognition or present recognition	33	36.7	Parent company	2	8.3
			Division	1	45.8

Parent company giving written advice or instruction on:	Manual	Non-manual	Per cent	Manual	Non-manual
facilities for trade unions	41.2	31.4		8.3	4.2
disclosure of information for collective bargaining	26.5	20.6		12.5	12.5
individual and collective grievance handling	58.8	54.9		20.8	20.8
handling of discipline	57.8	54.9		29.2	29.2
implementation of holiday arrangements	56.8	52.9		41.7	41.7
sick pay implementation	58.8	59.8		29.2	33.3
recruitment	39.2	34.3		12.5	16.7
selection	29.5	31.4		16.7	20.8
transfer	39.2	38.2		16.7	25.0

5.05b Written and unwritten advice to managers on employee relations practice from company or divisional head office: where trade unions are not recognised

	Multi-establishment company			Division of multi	
	Number	Per cent		Number	Per cent
Company or division recognising	12	11.8		5	17.2
Issuing written advice on attitudes to or action on recognition	2	16.7	Parent company	1	20.0
			Division	1	20.0
Giving unwritten advice on attitudes to or action on recognition	5	41.7	Parent company	2	40.0
			Division	1	20.0

Parent company giving written advice or instructions on:	Manual	Non-manual		Manual	Non-manual
			Per cent		
individual and collective grievance handling	41.7	41.7		80.0	80.0
handling of discipline	50.0	50.0		80.0	80.0
implementation of holiday arrangements	66.7	66.7		80.0	80.0
sick pay implementation	75.0	66.7		60.0	60.0
recruitment	25.0	25.0		60.0	60.0
selection	8.3	8.3		60.0	60.0
transfer	25.0	25.0		60.0	60.0

5.06 Method of obtaining the views of employees where no trade unions are recognised

	Multi-establishment company		Division of multi	
	Number	Per cent	Number	Per cent
Company or division not recognising	12	11.8	5	17.2
Obtain views of employees through:				
normal supervisory channels	8	66.7	3	60.0
day-to-day contact	7	58.3	3	60.0
open door policy	7	59.3	2	40.0
periodic discussion with employees	2	16.7	2	40.0
works (advisory) council	1	8.3	1	20.0
consultative committee	2	16.7	1	20.0
representative staff association	1	8.3	1	20.0

5.07 Consultation and communication: company and divisional head office

	Multi-establishment companies		Divisions of multis	
	Number	Per cent	Number	Per cent
Formal consultation				
works councils or committees of employees	25	24.5	38	21.6
works councils or committees of trade unionists	17	16.7	9	31.0
joint consultative committees	32	31.4	11	37.9
Informal consultation				
management practices	68	66.7	24	82.7
Briefing groups				
Used by management	33	32.5	10	34.5
began:				
1979	5	15.3	3	30.0
1978	6	18.3	1	10.0
1977	3	9.7	1	10.0
1971–1976	15	16.6	5	50.0
1965–1970	0	0.0	0	0.0
1960–1964	1	0.4	0	0.0
1955–1959	0	0.0	0	0.0
1950–1954	0	0.0	0	0.0
Before 1950	3	9.7	0	0.0
no response	0	0.0	0	0.0
	33	100.0	10	100.0

5.08 Employee reporting

Companies		Multi-establishment company		Division of multi	
		Number	Per cent	Number	Per cent
Issuing employee	HO	61	59.8	6	20.7
reports	Divs	NA	NA	7	24.1
Organising face-to face meetings to give financial information		68	66.7	19	65.5
Of which held:					
regularly		30	44.1	10	52.6
from time to time		38	55.9	9	47.4
			100.0		100.0
Encourage divisions to issue employee reports		32	31.4	–	–
Encourage establish-ments to issue employee reports		–	–	8	27.6

5.09   Company journal or newspaper

	Multi-establishment company		Division of multi	
	Number	Per cent	Number	Per cent
All situations in which journal or newspaper issued from head office:	57	55.9	15	51.7
Of which:				
for HO employees (company or division)	49	86.0	6	20.7
generally throughout company or division	55	96.5	15	51.7
Issued:				
weekly	0	0.0	0	0.0
monthly	26	45.6	7	46.7
quarterly	25	43.9	7	46.7
annually	4	7.0	0	0.0
irregularly	2	3.5	1	6.6
	57	100.0	15	100.0
Journals or newspapers also issued by:				
subsidiary companies or divisions:				
some	31	30.4	–	–
all	6	5.9	–	–
none or no response	65	63.7	–	–
particular establishments within divisions:				
some	–	–	4	13.8
all	–	–	4	13.8
none	–	–	21	72.4
	102	100.0	29	100.0

5.010 Company policy on consultation and participation at divisional and establishment levels where trade unions are to any extent recognised

	Multi-establishment company			Division of multi	
	Number	Per cent		Number	Per cent
Companies and divisions recognising trade unions	90	88.2		24	82.8
Companies in which:					
consultative arrangements exist in establishments	65	72.2		16	66.7
policy is to establish or to encourage:					
works councils	43	47.8	Parent company	4	16.7
			Division	11	45.8
joint consultative committees	56	62.2	Parent company	7	29.2
			Division	11	45.8
Companies with policies on participation beyond the use of consultation e.g.					
TU representation on boards of management committees	6	6.7		2	8.3
non-TU representatives on boards of management committees	8	8.9		2	8.3
representation of TUs or employees in:					
financial planning	3	3.3		1	4.2
marketing policy	4	4.4		0	0.0
selling policy	4	4.4		1	4.2
factory or plant development	20	22.2		4	16.6
product planning	9	10.0		3	12.5
other	12	13.3		2	8.3
Companies which have established or encourage briefing groups	35	38.9	Parent company	5	20.8
			Division	6	25.0
Companies which believe that briefing groups work satisfactorily	30	33.3		5	20.8

5.011 Policy on participation beyond the use of consultation where no trade unions are recognised

	Multi-establishment company		Division of multi	
	Number	Per cent	Number	Per cent
Representation of trade unions on board or management committee	0	0.0	0	0.0
Non-trade union representation on board or management committee	3	25.0	2	40.0
Representation of employees in:				
financial planning	0	0.0	0	0.0
marketing policy	2	16.7	0	0.0
selling policy	3	25.0	0	0.0
factory development	4	33.3	1	20.0
product planning	3	25.0	1	20.0
other	1	8.3	1	20.0

	Multi-establishment company		Division of multi	
	Number	Per cent	Number	Per cent
Discussed by company main board	61	59.8	7	24.1
Not discussed by main board	30	29.4	14	48.3
Don't know and no response	11	10.8	8	27.6
If not discussed, other action taken	13	12.7	3	10.3
Division received from company head office:				
instructions	–	–	0	0.0
advice	–	–	2	6.9
neither instruction nor advice	–	–	17	58.6
no response	–	–	10	34.5
	–	–	29	100.0

6 Pay levels and determination

The background

During a period of intermittent incomes policies, discussion of pay in the 1960s became focused principally on the twin issues of 'drift' and 'productivity bargaining', the latter encouraging the development of deals which would link wage increases with improved labour utilisation and the former drawing attention to systems of payment, particularly those involving payment by results, which had developed symptoms of running out of control at workshop level. Both the attack on drift and the encouragement of productivity bargaining involved the notion that managements ought, both in the interests of their companies and of the economy, to display initiative in strengthening relationships between pay and performance, thereby also improving the state of management control by the more careful selection of appropriate pay systems and/or methods of measuring performance. In relation to the former, there was much speculation about the use of controlled or measured daywork, while pursuit of the latter brought a boom in industrial engineering.

Greater attention to pay *systems* and the need for management initiative extended the argument to *structures* of pay, first by drawing attention to the role of differentials in determining the acceptability and stability of settlements, and second by opening up questions of pay bargaining levels. The differentials issue led in many cases to the more thorough structuring of pay through job grading and job evaluation, particularly for non-manual employees. The issue of bargaining levels was taken up by the Donovan Commission as part of its approach to the

150

restructuring of employee relations as a whole. The Commission saw the problem of such relations in the 1950s and 1960s as arising from the failure of national (or industry-wide) agreements between trade unions and employers associations established over the previous half-century effectively to regulate the great body of *domestic bargaining* which full-employment and other factors had engendered in British factories. In the words of Allan Flanders, whose thinking on the matter so greatly influenced the Commission's report, the 'formal' system represented by such agreements had been overtaken by workplace arrangements which were 'largely informal, largely fragmented and largely autonomous'. It followed that there was an urgent need to remedy the 'central defect [in the British system] of disorder in factory and workshop relations and pay structures promoted by the conflict between the formal and informal systems' which could not be 'accomplished by employers' associations and trade unions working at industry level or by industry-wide agreements'. *Factory-wide* agreements were, the Commission believed, the answer to the problem. These could succeed where industry-wide agreements had failed, putting payment systems into their context, settling differentials and establishing realistic procedures for their own enforcement. *Company level* agreements might, the Commission thought, serve a similar purpose where 'boards of companies . . . prefer to negotiate company agreements rather than allow each factory manager to negotiate separately on his own'. Whichever level was preferred, boards were recommended 'to develop, together with trade unions representative of their employees, comprehensive and authoritative collective bargaining machinery to deal at company and/or factory level with terms and conditions of employment that are settled at these levels'.

Since 1968, when the Commission reported, a number of inquiries have sought to establish what changes have subsequently taken place in British payment systems and structures. What follows is a summary of the contribution which the present survey appears to make to the debate. It should be noted that the Commission prepared no detailed account of the role of industry-wide agreements nor, in general, about the state of play at the time of its report. Any attempt to measure the extent of change since that time is therefore, to a considerable extent, speculative.

The role of industry-wide agreements

The Donovan Commission gravely distorted the role and status of industry-wide agreements in its attempt to show that conventional relationships had broken down under pressure of workplace bargaining. Some industries' agreements at industry-wide level at that time continued to provide effective external regulation of pay and conditions; in others, such as engineering, this had never been their objective except in the case of certain standard conditions of work. Such agreements provided minima and were widely influential in having their percentage or monetary increases in basic rates applied by firms. There was, undoubtedly, an increase in effectiveness of 'domestic' bargaining in many industries especially from the point at which shop steward organisation began an effective revival from the middle of the 1950s, but this did not necessarily represent a challenge to industry-wide agreements; the erosion was gradual.

Undoubtedly that erosion has continued. In some industries the one-time regulatory force of industry-wide agreements has almost wholly broken down. Those in biscuits, chocolate and confectionery will serve as examples. In others, such as letterpress printing, unions are commonly thought to insist on increases or improvements from industry-wide agreements being universally applied. In engineering, and in some other industries, minimum earnings levels are all that are required to be observed so far as manual workers' pay in general is concerned, although companies also undoubtedly apply them in other ways. The situation varies from one set of circumstances to another. For many companies there is effectively no industry-wide level of pay for manuals; in some, national pay increases are always or sometimes followed. For non-manuals there has never existed in most circumstances an industry-wide agreement, but firms can hardly act without consideration of what is happening to manual workers in all cases.

Companies responding to the survey were asked whether they applied improvements in industry-wide agreements in determining pay and conditions for manual and non-manual employees (6.3 and 6.02a and b). About one-third of headquarters and divisions of multis said that it was their practice 'never' to do so and one-third that they 'always' did so where manual workers were concerned; 20 per cent replied that they sometimes did so. For individual establishments taken as a whole, the corresponding figures were 8 per cent 'never', 48 per cent 'always' and 38 per cent 'sometimes'. Manual worker agreements at national level appear, therefore, to have a considerable effect on pay determination for non-manuals, especially at establishment level. The percentage of situations in which such agreements were *not* applied by headquarters and divisions was about the same as for manuals at those levels. The corresponding 'always' and 'sometimes' figure was also lower (about one-third). Establishments, however, reported that they 'always or sometimes' applied industry-wide agreements in three-quarters of all cases at that level.

It seems that national agreements, although they may nowadays very infrequently form the sole basis for workplace settlements in manufacturing, continue to exercise considerable influence. In the survey that influence showed no particular pattern so far as industry or size of company was concerned. Willingness to apply national agreements 'always' or 'sometimes' appeared to occur quite randomly over the survey companies. No doubt each company was influenced by its own history, custom and practice and by the attitudes of unions (if any), among other things. It would, however, seem that the nearer to the establishment level, the more likely national agreements will be applied.

The extent of negotiation

It is far from easy to measure the extent to which pay and conditions are negotiated. The word 'negotiated' has no precise meaning and there may be differences of opinion between representatives of management and employees on some occasions on whether particular items have been negotiated or mutually agreed or not. In any particular establishment some groups of employees may have their terms and conditions determined by negotiation (however defined) while others, whether organised or not, simply follow suit. Alternatively, some terms may be arrived at by negotiation and others not, or some employee groups be subject to bargained settlements while the pay and/or conditions of others are determined unilaterally by management. Many companies exist in which there is no negotiation about terms and conditions at all. Some of these situations involve an element of consultation with the employees concerned or with their representatives, thereby raising the question whether such a process may, depending on circumstances, be regarded as a kind of 'bargaining' or whether staff are simply being informed of managerial decisions. In multi-establishment companies a combination of some or all of these situations may be found within the same organisation. Because of this last named difficulty, the survey information relates to single establishment companies, establishments of multis and the *headquarters employees* only of multi establishment companies, whether head office or divisional.

Over 35 per cent of single establishment companies reported that they determined the pay of their manual workers unilaterally, 31 per cent that they did so by agreement with employee representatives and 34 per cent that they used a combination of these methods (6.1a). Where they claimed to negotiate manual worker pay at their level, establishments of multis were more involved in negotiation; only 24 per cent noted that they determined pay unilaterally (6.01a). They were, of course, more likely to recognise trade unions than single establishment companies. In both types of company, conditions of work were less likely to be negotiated than pay (6.1b). Where non-manual employees were concerned, unilateral determination of both pay and conditions was higher than for manual employees (6.01b).

For the headquarters staff of multi-establishment companies, unilateral determination of pay for non-manual employees was somewhat more common than at single establishment companies and very much more common than at establishments of multis; divisional headquarters showed a similar picture and this was replicated at both levels so far as conditions were concerned (6.01a and b). Trade unions appear to have had limited effect in headquarter staff situations. This is also true for manual workers. 28 per cent of headquarters of multis and 21 per cent of headquarters of divisions reported having no such workers. Where they had such workers, about one-half of them reported negotiating on pay and conditions. Tables 6A and 6B show no clear pattern of non-negotiation by category of worker either for pay or conditions at headquarters of multis.

Systems and structures of payment

The form of the survey did not make it possible to determine with any precision whether or not companies had taken heed of the advice prevalent in the 1960s and 1970s to select and control more carefully their wage payment systems and to improve their pay structures. At establishment level, individual piecework for manual workers was to be found in one-quarter of single establishment companies but was somewhat less common where establishments of multis were concerned (6.4). Group piecework was somewhat less popular. Both types of establishment applied it to semi-skilled workers (in 18 and 15 per cent of cases respectively), but single establishment companies were for some reason more likely to apply it to skilled and unskilled workers than establishments of multis. High day rate systems, except where skilled workers were concerned, proved to be more common (but only in about one company in ten) in single establishment companies. Value added systems, vigorously advocated in some quarters in the 1970s, appear to have found converts in 4 or 5 per cent of instances only. The general impression is that, so far as systems of payment are concerned, the situation has changed very little. It may be that establishments changing their systems in one direction (e.g. towards day work) have been offset by other establishments moving in the opposite direction (e.g. towards piecework or some other form of payment by results). Bonus systems of one kind or another continue to prevail.

Table 6A
Method of establishing pay by category of employee
Headquarters of multi-establishment companies

Manual For:	By unilateral decision	After consultation	By agreement	All methods
		Number of companies		
All manual employees	2	6	20	28
Catering and maintenance	7	4	9	20
Craftsmen and general service electricians and bricklayers	0	2	0	2
Drivers and warehouse	0	1	0	1
TGWU/AUEW/NGA/NATSOPA	0	0	1	1
Operatives/tradesmen	0	0	5	5
Drivers, fitters etc.	1	0	0	1
Drivers/plant works	0	0	3	3
Mostly consult	0	1	0	1
No manual workers	0	0	0	29
No detailed response	4	7	0	11
Totals	14	21	38	102

Non-manual				
All non-manual employees	14	8	7	29
Management/admin./clerical	13	0	0	13
Non-exec./clerical/professional/ administration/security	1	0	0	1
Senior and middle management	0	1	0	1
Management/clerical/technical	0	0	7	7
Office staff	1	0	0	1
Clerical/admin./management	0	4	0	4
Clerical/sen. eng.	0	0	1	1
Staff association	0	0	1	1
Management/technical/clerical	0	3	1	4
Clerical/admin.	0	10	10	20
Directors/executive/clerical	0	2	0	2
No detailed response	8	4	3	15
No response	0	0	0	1
Totals	37	32	32	102

Table 6B
Method of establishing pay by category of employee
Headquarters of division of multi-establishment companies

Manual For:	By unilateral decision	After consultation	By agreement	All methods
		Number of companies		
All manual employees	2	2	10	14
Security/maintenance	1	0	1	2
Packers	1	0	0	1
Maintenance/drivers/garage packers	0	1	0	1
All service & associated engineering	0	1	0	1
Hourly semi-skilled, tradesmen and technicians	0	1	0	1
Technicians/auxiliary workers	0	0	1	1
General process/craft	0	0	1	1
Supervisors	0	0	1	1
No manual workers	0	0	0	6
Totals	4	5	14	29

Non-manual	By unilateral decision	After consultation	By agreement	All methods
All non-manual employees	8	4	1	13
Managerial/clerical	1	2	0	3
Admin./technical/clerical	0	2	0	2
Clerical/junior admin.	0	0	1	1
Clerical/technical	0	0	3	3
Supervision/commercial/laboratory/technical	0	0	1	1
Staff association	0	0	1	1
Clerical/admin./middle mgrs.	0	0	2	2
No detailed response	2	1	0	3
Totals	11	9	9	29

There can be little doubt, however, that job grading and evaluation for manual workers have begun to take hold.[1] About one-third of single establishment companies and one-half of establishments of multis operated one structural device or the other and this proportion was, as might be expected, maintained or increased where non-manual workers were concerned. A surprising proportion of non-manual workers also participated in bonus schemes of some kind—20 per cent in single establishment companies and nearer 30 per cent in establishments of multis.

Head offices of multis and headquarters of divisions vary very considerably in their attitudes towards laying down from their levels pay structures or systems for their individual establishments. Unquestionably they have exercised some influence in the direction of more common and orderly arrangements but the extent to which they have done so remains difficult to determine. The survey shows that about one-third claim to have systems and/or structures for manual workers which are common to *all* their establishments and about one-half make the same claim in respect of non-manual workers (6.06a—c). Smaller percentages (14 to 20 per cent approximately) of such companies claim, at one level or another, to have systems and structures common to different groups at *some* of their establishments. This does not prove that they are moving towards greater uniformity as and when this is possible, but such a conclusion might reasonably be inferred in some cases.

Levels of bargaining

The Donovan prescription required factory or company-wide agreements negotiated by 'comprehensive and authoritative' collective bargaining machinery at these levels. The exact significance of such words and phrases was never clear. 'Factory-wide' and 'company-wide' presumably meant that agreements were to be concluded at works director or most senior manager or director level in each case (i.e. that they should *not* be, in engineering terminology, merely 'domestically' negotiated *ad hoc* on the shop floor). But did this also imply that only a *single* agreement (or at most two, perhaps, one for manuals and one for non-manuals) was being advised? Or could a number of agreements be concluded within the recommended formula? Was the word 'comprehensive' intended to apply to the range of *coverage* of the agreement(s), or to *content*, or to both coverage and content? What did

1 The Warwick survey (see Brown, William, 1981, p.111) presents a not too dissimilar picture of the situation. It also notes that 34 per cent of the establishments with job evaluation had increased their coverage in the past five years. Between 50 and 70 per cent of the companies in the present survey (depending on type) claimed to have reviewed or reconstructed wage and salary systems in 1979 (see p.114).

'authoritative' mean; that the parties had authority to negotiate or that the agreements ought to be well negotiated and hence well founded, or did it mean that both characteristics were necessary? One thing only appears to be clear in the Donovan prescription: the Commission surely intended that agreements should be *in writing*.

Such a complex of uncertainties and ambiguities makes it impossible, at least by survey methods, to collect information which will show, beyond all doubt, whether there had been since 1968 a discernible move towards the Donovan formula or not. From the present inquiry very few written agreements were presented which could claim to be 'comprehensive'. Of those that were submitted, most were from prominent companies and were well known to us already. This does not mean to say that other companies covered by the survey could not have produced such agreements had they wished to do so, but it does suggest that such agreements were not uppermost in their thinking. Very few, it clearly emerged, had *consolidated* their agreements, i.e. had reviewed their written but 'fragmented' agreements or understandings at plant or 'domestic' level and put these together in a single volume. Annual settlements had, however, become common, especially since the middle 1960s.[1] But informal domestic bargaining was clearly continuing in many factories and the 'authority' of these settlements in any Donovan sense may well be questionable. While there is very likely to be more written material containing agreements on display in factories than was once the case, we are therefore unable to say what progress had been made in a 'Donovan direction'. If pressed, we would have to say that we believe that this has been modest.

What then can be said about the suggestion that, within the spirit of the Donovan recommendations there may have grown up in multi-establishment companies a movement towards *company-wide* or *divisional level* agreements? On this we have evidence from individual establishments of multis (6.2) and from divisional and head office levels of multis, albeit for the most part of different companies from those to which the individual establishments relate (6.02). This evidence may appear to be contradictory. For both manual and non-manual employees over 80 per cent of individual establishments see themselves as determining pay and conditions independently of their parent company; head offices of multis see themselves as determining pay for manual workers at *all* divisions and establishments in about one-quarter of cases, and at *some* divisions and establishments at almost one-quarter also, with similar figures for non-manual workers.

It may be that establishments of multis are inclined to maintain that they have more independence from their head offices than these head

1 Before that time few agreements had termination dates.

158

offices would ascribe to them or that head offices themselves may claim more authority than is their due. A detailed examination of the 24 multi-establishment companies which recorded that they determined the pay of manual workers at all divisions and establishments showed that these fell into five categories. First there were those who regarded the application of an industry-wide agreement (typically an industry-wide JIC agreement in the negotiation of which the company had presumably taken part) as a 'company' agreement. Of these there were five, employing in total 11,200 employees. In all cases the industry-wide rates applied were regarded as minima and it was thought proper to remove these from the 'central bargaining' category.

Three other types of central bargaining also seemed questionable in the Donovan sense, principally because the central bargaining function described appeared to have arisen more as a result of chance and circumstances than because of consideration of the bargaining structure itself. One company, with a principal factory in which negotiations took place with trade unions, applied the results of these negotiations directly and unilaterally to a non-union subsidiary several hundred miles away. A second type had arisen where, for purposes of financial control, company operations on a single site had been broken down into separate accounting units with limited liability company status, leaving the whole site to be treated as one unit for wage determination purposes. Thirdly, there were those companies in which the subsidiaries noted were no more than operational branches of headquarters.

If these types of central bargaining are discounted for present purposes, 11 companies only appear to practise company-wide bargaining for manual workers in one of three ways. Some, like Ford, operate a joint industrial council type bargaining structure, under whatever name, sometimes involving shop stewards only and sometimes full-time trade union officials, or officials *and* shop stewards. In others, a single dominant union negotiates, in effect, for all employees, whether members of this union or not. A third appears to involve no formal co-operation between unions, the common factor being the management negotiator who ensures a common settlement between factories.

Even in these cases, the degree of coverage and control exercised by the company bargain appears to vary. In the most comprehensive cases, company bargaining was accompanied by company-wide pay structures based on grading or job evaluation; in others, there was clearly room for some element of negotiation about bonus and other matters at works or factory level. Indeed, some of those companies in the survey which recorded that they did *not* determine pay and conditions for all employees at company level appeared to exercise more direct regulation from that level than some of those which said that they did.

As might be expected, a larger number of companies considered that they determined manual workers conditions from head office level (6.03a), although the same could not be said for the pay of non-manual employees (6.02a), reflecting the development of bargaining at lower levels with staff unions, principally ASTMS. The same consideration was, however, reflected in the case of non-manual employees conditions (6.03b).

In situations in which head office multis leave divisions and establishments substantially free to negotiate at divisional or works level, and on items which fall outside head office negotiations, the co-ordination of settlements may become a matter of some importance. This may become more significant as a problem if companies, as a number suggested in the survey, are pursuing a deliberate policy of decentralising their bargaining arrangements. In practice, co-ordination is seldom absent, even in companies which attempt to practise considerable centralisation, and merely tails off as less centralisation is attempted, rather than disappearing altogether. A good deal may depend on the degree of seriousness with which headquarters management regards the issue of standardisation of payment systems of structures at lower levels in the company.

Co-ordination methods are clearly related to the nature of the organisation of the company for employee relations purposes and to preferred styles as well as to payment systems and structures. In those companies with full- or part-time employee relations specialists at head office level, and particularly in those with employee relations sub committees, there is a natural tendency to use such machinery, or special *ad hoc* meetings arranged within it, for co-ordination purposes. Indeed, such activity may be its principal rationale. Such an approach has been encouraged by the practice of annual reviews which has evidently been on the increase since the middle 1960s (6.03, 6.04, 6.06). In other situations, companies refer to 'central personnel overview', 'liaison with HQ', 'liaison through central personnel department', or, more elaborately, to 'checks and balances through group personnel to maintain consistency and equitable standards of pay, pay increases and other changes to terms and conditions through consultative meetings between personnel and executives'. Such executive meetings, with or without personnel specialists, appear to be reasonably common. Where, however, the strength of the chief executive dominates the company, co-ordination could be summarised by our respondents in two words—'all conform'!

In the cases in which comparatively loose control is exercised, it may simply be that, without any detailed criteria from head office, 'lower level settlements need head office approval'. Other companies 'set negotiating targets', limits or norms. There appears to be no general practice on such matters. A simple system where companies are relatively small and establishments or divisions limited in number is for one person from, or through, head office, to be responsible for and possibly for the conduct of, all negotiations. Much more detail would be required than can be obtained from a general employee relations survey of this kind to establish trends and development in this area, but it is evident that there can be few multi-establishment companies which have by this time failed to provide for co-ordination on pay and conditions claims of some kind, whether simple or complex in character. No doubt this is one reason why such negotiations and their possible consequences are likely to be discussed by main boards more frequently than most other employee relations issues. They lend themselves, of course, compared with many other issues in employee relations, to quantitative treatment and this may also add to their attraction from the board point of view, both in relation to costs and to pricing policies.

Summary

1. Although negotiation with trade unions predominates in the determination of pay and conditions of work, unilateral determination by employers, with or without consultation, is not unusual in companies of all kinds where some or all employees are concerned. Undoubtedly, as the Warwick inquiry found, the absence of negotiations is 'significantly more common in [smaller establishments] and in single plant as opposed to multi plant establishments'.[1] The smaller size of many of our establishments and possibly the emphasis which the present survey places on single establishment companies may account for the greater 'abstention' from bargaining that we have revealed. This increases for conditions as distinct from pay, and for non-manual workers generally. At the headquarters of multi-establishment companies collective bargaining is, for a variety of reasons, less prevalent for both manual and non-manual workers even than among single establishment companies.

2. Industry-wide agreements appear to be alive and well, not in the sense in which they once operated in some industries of providing a unique basis for pay and conditions, but in the sense that the improvements in pay and conditions provided in them continue to be widely applied in manufacturing, sometimes on an invariable and sometimes on a from-time-to-time basis, and especially at establishment level. If

1 Brown, W. (1981) p.7. 17 per cent of the Warwick establishments employing 50—100 employees were *not* involved in bargaining; no establishment employing more than 1,000 was in this position — Table 2.2, p.9. The Warwick data (pp.7—13) is at no point compatible with our own in the way in which it handles 'multi-employer bargaining'.

industry-wide agreements have ceased in some respects to be regulative, they remain influential, directly or indirectly, for both manual and non-manual employees.

3. The overall pattern of systems of pay used in manufacturing establishments appears to be as variable as ever. Despite much publicity, high day rate and value added systems have probably made little progress. On the other hand, job grading and evaluation have established themselves and may have been further extended in the 1970s.[1]

4. Annual pay reviews have become increasingly common since the 1960s and early 1970s, a development which can easily be underestimated in the advance towards the more systematic treatment of employee relations by companies.

5. There is no evidence of more than a moderate movement in the 'Donovan' direction of 'comprehensive and authoritative agreements' at plant and/or company levels, if by this is meant agreements which are both consolidated, wide ranging in coverage and content and systematically policed and administered at lower levels.

6. Company-wide bargaining, strictly defined, is practised by only about one-in-ten of multi-establishment companies. In some cases divisional level bargaining exists in addition, or as an alternative. It seems likely that there has been no significant move towards company-wide bargaining in British manufacturing as described and defined in the survey, although there has undoubtedly been a development of *partial* bargaining and even more head office involvement in settlements at lower levels, if only as a result of incomes policies and financial imperatives. Some evidence in the survey suggests that companies have been actively decentralising their bargaining to establishment level, reserving for themselves at head office a role as co-ordinator rather than direct bargainer.[2]

1. Brown, W., ibid., p.114.
2. It seems inevitable that comparisons will be made with the Warwick inquiry on these points. The Warwick data on bargaining levels was derived from questions relating to the last pay settlement in each establishment under one or other of the phases of incomes policy which may have been relevant in each case. The question concerned asked whether the appropriate settlement was *affected* by a Wages Council, an industry-wide agreement, regional or district negotiation, a company, divisional, or establishment bargain, in so far as the largest part of the increase was concerned (pp.133-4). It is possible to interpret this question as unrelated to the company or industry questioned in any direct sense and some respondents may have done so. Nevertheless, on the 'corporate' level of agreement, the results are not too dissimilar from our own, the 'most important level' being corporate in 11.3 per cent for manual workers and 14.9 per cent for non-manual workers (Tables 2.1 and 2.3). The writers go on to suggest, however, that there has been an increase in 'corporate agreements' (p.11). The argument is a complex one based in part on the observation that 'the opportunity to have a corporate agreement increases with establishment size' but also defining 'corporate' to refer to 'agreements which cover *more than one, but not necessarily all*, establishments in a multi-establishment firm. The latter consideration would seem to be the more important from the point of view of comparison with our data. Can relevance to a single subsidiary establishment be said to establish the existence of company bargaining? If such a relaxation were applied to this survey, some 46 per cent of headquarters of multis could claim to be the bargaining level for their manual and non-manual employees.

References

Brown, W.A. and Terry, M.A. 'The Changing Nature of National Wage Agreements', *Scottish Journal of Political Economy*, Vol.XXV, No.2, 1978.

Brown, W. 'The Structure of Pay Bargaining in Britain', Paper prepared for *Conference on the Pay Bargaining System*, Chatham House, 25–26 June 1980.

Brown, W. (ed.) *Changing Contours of British Industrial Relations*, Basil Blackwell, 1981.

Commission on Industrial Relations. *Industrial Relations in Multi-Plant Undertakings*, Report No.85, HMSO, 1974.

Daniel, W.W., *Wage Determination in Industry*, (Political and Economic Planning), Vol.XLII, No.563, 1976.

Deaton, D.R. and Beaumont, P.B. 'The Determinants of Bargaining Structure: Some Large Scale Survey Evidence for Britain', *British Journal of Industrial Relations*, Vol.XVIII, No.2, 1980.

Fox, Alan and Flanders, Allan. 'The Reform of Collective Bargaining: From Donovan to Durkheim', *British Journal of Industrial Relations*, Vol.7, No.2, July 1969.

Greenberg, David F. 'The Structures of Collective Bargaining and some of its Determinants', *Proceedings of the Industrial Relations Research Association*, Winter 1966.

Lindop, Esmond. Workplace Bargaining – the end of an era? *Industrial Relations Journal*, Vol.10, No.1, Spring 1979.

National Board for Prices and Incomes, *Job Evaluation*, Report No.83, Cmnd.3772, HMSO, 1968.

Ramsey, J.C. 'Negotiating in a Multi-Plant Company', *Industrial Relations Journal*, Vol.2, No.2, Summer 1971.

Roberts, B.C. and Gennard, J. 'Trends in Plant and Company Bargaining', *Scottish Journal of Political Economy*, Vol.XVII, No.2, June 1970.

Royal Commission on Trade Unions and Employers' Associations, 1965–68, Cmnd. 3623, June 1968. Report.

Shister, Joseph. 'Collective Bargaining' in Neil W. Chamberlain et al. (eds.), *A Decade of Industrial Relations Research, 1946–1956*, Harper and Row, 1958.

Terry, Michael. 'The Inevitable Growth of Informality', *British Journal of Industrial Relations*, Vol.XV, No.1, March 1977.

Thomson, A.W.J. and Hunter, L.C. 'The Level of Bargaining in a Multi-Plant Company', *Industrial Relations Journal*, Vol.6, No.2, Summer 1975.

Thomson, Andrew and Gregory, Mary. 'British Bargaining Structure and its Impact on Pay'. *Personnel Management*, December 1980.

Tabulations

Pay levels and determination

6.1a Establishing terms and conditions of work

Manual workers—pay

Terms and conditions determined	Single establishment company		Individual establishment multi	
	Number	Per cent	Number	Per cent
By unilateral management decision	20	12.8	5	10.9
After consultation	35	22.4	6	13.0
By agreement with employee representatives	48	30.8	15	32.6
By a combination of any or all above	53	34.0	20	43.5
	156	100.0	46*	100.0

Manual workers—conditions

By unilateral management decision	15	9.7	2	4.3
After consultation	47	30.3	8	17.0
By agreement with employee representatives	38	24.5	14	29.8
By a combination of any or all above	55	35.5	23	48.9
	155	100.0	47*	100.0

* Representing establishments in which pay and conditions are determined at establishment level; in the balance of instances, divisional or headquarters are the levels at which pay and conditions are determined.

164

6.1b Establishing terms and conditions of work

Non-manual workers—pay

	Single establishment company		Individual establishment multi	
	Number	Per cent	Number	Per cent
By unilateral management decision	37	23.9	9	20.5
After consultation	57	36.8	8	18.2
By agreement with employee representatives	17	11.0	13	29.5
By a combination of any or all above	44	28.3	14	31.8
	155	100.0	44*	100.0

Non-manual workers—conditions

	Single establishment company		Individual establishment multi	
By unilateral management decision	24	15.6	5	11.4
After consultation	72	46.7	10	22.7
By agreement with employee representatives	14	9.1	14	31.8
By a combination of any or all above	44	28.6	15	34.1
	154	100.0	44*	100.0

* See note Table 6.1a.

6.2 Levels of determination of pay and conditions

Individual establishments—multi. Pay

	Manual employees		Non-manual employees	
	Number	Per cent	Number	Per cent
Establishment	46	85.2	44	81.5
Division	4	7.4	6	11.1
Parent company	2	3.7	4	7.4
No response	2	3.7	–	–
	54	100.0	54	100.0

Individual establishments—multi. Conditions

	Number	Per cent	Number	Per cent
Establishment	47	87.0	44	81.5
Division	4	7.4	6	11.1
Parent company	1	1.9	4	7.4
No response	2	3.7	–	–
	54	100.0	54	100.0

6.3 Application of improvements in appropriate national collective agreements in determining terms and conditions of work

Manual

	Single establishment company		Individual establishment multi	
	Number	Per cent	Number	Per cent
Always	79	50.6	22	40.7
Sometimes	58	37.2	23	42.6
Never	11	7.1	5	9.3
No response	8	5.1	4	7.4
	156	100.0	54	100.0

Non-manual

Always	57	36.5	10	18.5
Sometimes	60	38.5	24	44.5
Never	20	12.8	10	18.5
No response	19	12.2	10 .	18.5
	156	100.0	54	100.0

6.4 Pay systems and structures

Manual

	Single establishment company			Individual establishment multi		
	Skilled	Semi-skilled	Un-skilled	Skilled	Semi-skilled	Un-skilled
			Per cent			
Individual piecework	25.7	26.3	15.4	16.7	22.2	10.1
Group piecework	14.8	18.0	13.5	7.4	14.9	3.7
High day rate	13.4	11.4	7.0	18.6	1.9	1.9
Value added system	4.5	5.1	5.1	3.7	3.7	3.7
Job evaluation	15.3	16.7	12.2	18.5	24.1	22.2
Job grading	16.6	13.4	11.5	22.2	27.8	25.9
Other bonus etc.	26.9	28.8	28.8	37.0	40.7	38.9

Non-manual

	Clerical	Technical	Admin.	Clerical	Technical	Admin.
Individual piecework	0.0	0.6	0.0	0.0	0.0	0.0
Group piecework	0.6	0.0	0.0	0.0	0.0	0.0
High day rate	12.0	10.9	11.5	9.3	9.3	7.4
Value added system	5.1	4.5	4.5	3.7	3.7	3.7
Job evaluation	16.6	16.0	16.6	32.2	33.3	35.0
Job grading	15.4	13.5	14.7	22.4	18.5	20.4
Other bonus etc.	19.8	20.5	20.4	27.8	27.8	31.5

168

6.01a Establishing terms and conditions of work: company and divisional head office staff

Manual workers—pay

Terms and conditions determined	Multi-establishment company		Division of multi	
	Number	Per cent	Number	Per cent
By unilateral management decision	14	13.7	4	13.8
After consultation	21	20.6	5	17.2
By agreement with employee representatives	38	37.3	14	48.3
No manual workers or no response	29	28.4	6	20.7
	102	100.0	29	100.0

Manual workers—conditions

By unilateral management decision	13	12.7	4	13.8
After consultation	24	23.5	5	17.2
By agreement with employee representatives	36	35.3	14	48.3
No manual workers or no response	29	28.4	6	23.7
	102	100.0	29	100.0

6.01b Establishing terms and conditions of work: company and divisional head office staff

Non manual workers—pay

	Multi-establishment company		Division of multi	
	Number	Per cent	Number	Per cent
By unilateral management decision	37	36.3	11	37.9
After consultation	32	31.4	9	31.0
By agreement with employee representatives	32	31.4	9	31.0
No response	1	1.0	0	0.0
	102	100.0	29	100.0

Non-manual workers—conditions

	Number	Per cent	Number	Per cent
By unilateral management decision	35	34.3	10	34.5
After consultation	34	33.3	11	37.9
By agreement with employee representatives	32	31.4	8	27.6
No response	1	1.0	0	0.0
	102	100.0	29	100.0

6.02a Pay determination from head office and division: manual employees

	Multi-establishment company		Division of multi	
	Number	Per cent	Number	Per cent
Head office negotiates regularly on pay for:	47	46.1 (52.2)	8	27.6 (33.3)
All divisions and establishments	24	51.1	2	25.0
Some divisions and establishments	23	48.9	6	75.0
	47	100.0	8	100.0
Head office negotiates on:				
basic pay	11	23.4	3	37.5
basic pay + bonus	31	66.0	3	37.5
no response	5	10.6	2	25.0
Head office does not negotiate	55	53.9	21	72.4
Of which cases:				
head office determines pay for all unilaterally or after consultation	11	20.0	5	23.8
head office determines pay for some unilaterally or after consultation	15	27.3	NK	–
divisional head office negotiates for all establishments	NK	–	10	47.6
Divisions determine pay unilaterally for some groups	14	(15.5)	–	
Establishments determine pay unilaterally for some groups	10	(11.1)	–	
Improvements in relevant national agreements applied:				
always	34	33.3	16	55.2
sometimes	20	19.6	5	17.2
never	36	35.3	5	17.2

( ) Indicates n = 90 companies or 24 divisions recognising TUs.

171

6.02b Pay determination from head office and division: non-manual employees

	Multi-establishment company		Division of multi	
	Number	Per cent	Number	Per cent
Head office negotiates regularly on pay for:	47	46.1 (67.1)	10	34.5 (58.8)
all divisions and establishments	21	44.7	1	10.0
some divisions and establishments	15	31.9	5	50.0
some groups	11	23.4	4	40.0
	47	100.0	10	100.0
Head office negotiates on:				
basic pay	28	59.6	4	40.0
basic pay + bonus	19	40.4	2	20.0
Head office does not negotiate	55	53.9	19	65.5
Of which cases:				
head office determines pay for all unilaterally or after consultation	25	45.5	4	21.0
head office determines pay for some unilaterally or after consultation	30	54.5	NK	–
division head office negotiates for all establishments	NK	–	10	52.6
Divisions determine pay unilaterally for some groups	34	(48.6)	NK	–
Establishments determine pay unilaterally for some groups	27	(38.6)	NK	–
Improvements in relevant national agreements applied:				
always	16	15.7	12	41.4
sometimes	20	19.6	4	13.8
never	34	33.3	7	24.1

( ) Indicates n = 70 companies or 17 divisions recognising TUs.

6.03a Conditions of work determined from company head office: manual employees

	Multi-establishment company		Division of multi	
	Number	Per cent	Number	Per cent
Head office determines at:				
all divisions or establishments	45	44.1	7	24.1
some divisions or establishments	32	31.4	6	20.7
	77	100.0	13	100.0
Of which:				
holidays	72	93.5	12	92.3
overtime rates	58	75.3	8	61.5
pensions	69	89.6	12	92.3
sick pay	63	81.8	8	61.5
fringe benefits	65	84.4	9	69.2
Head office does not determine	25	(24.5)	16	(55.2)
attempts to co-ordinate	35	(34.3)	10	(34.5)
Head office reviews annually	34	(33.3)	12	(41.4)
practice began:				
1979	2	5.9	0	0.0
1978	1	2.9	0	0.0
1977	0	0.0	1	8.3
1971–1976	7	20.6	5	41.8
1965–1970	10	29.5	1	8.3
1960–1964	1	2.9	0	0.0
1955–1959	1	2.9	1	8.3
1950–1954	0	0.0	1	8.3
Before 1950	3	8.8	2	16.7
No response	9	26.5	1	8.3

( ) Percentages of total samples of 102 multi-establishment companies and 29 divisions.

6.03b Conditions of work determined from company head office: non-manual employees

	Multi-establishment company		Division of multi	
	Number	Per cent	Number	Per cent
Head office determines at:				
all divisions or establishments	58	56.9	7	58.9
some divisions or establishments	21	20.6	5	41.7
	79	100.0	12	100.0
Of which:				
holidays	77	97.5	11	91.7
overtime rates	65	82.2	9	75.2
pensions	78	98.7	11	91.7
sick pay	75	94.9	8	66.7
fringe benefits	76	96.2	8	66.7
Head office does not determine	23	(22.5)	17	(58.6)
attempts to co-ordinate	34	(33.3)	8	(27.6)
Head office reviews annually	28	(27.4)	14	(48.3)
practice began:				
1979	0	0.0	0	0.0
1978	1	3.6	0	0.0
1977	1	3.6	0	0.0
1971–1976	6	21.4	2	14.3
1965–1970	7	25.0	2	14.3
1960–1964	3	10.7	4	28.6
1955–1959	1	3.6	1	7.1
1950–1954	0	0.0	2	14.3
Before 1950	1	3.6	1	7.1
No response	8	28.5	2	14.3

( ) Percentages of total samples of 101 multi-establishment companies and 29 divisions.

	Manual		Non-manual	
	Number	Per cent	Number	Per cent
Divisional head office determines at:				
all establishments	16	72.7	18	81.8
some establishments	6	27.3	4	18.2
	22	100.0	22	100.0
Of which:				
holidays	19	86.4	20	90.9
overtime rates	18	81.8	19	86.4
pensions	15	68.2	13	59.1
sick pay	16	72.7	14	63.6
fringe benefits	16	72.7	18	81.8
Divisional head office does not determine	6	(20.7)	3	(10.3)
attempts to co-ordinate	5	(17.2)	3	(10.3)
Division reviews annually	11	(37.9)	12	(41.4)
practice began:				
1979	0	0.0	0	0.0
1978	0	0.0	0	0.0
1977	0	0.0	0	0.0
1971–1976	5	45.4	2	16.7
1965–1970	2	18.2	2	16.7
1960–1964	1	9.1	4	33.3
1955–1959	0	0.0	1	8.3
1950–1954	1	9.1	2	16.7
Before 1950	2	18.2	1	8.3

( ) Per cent of total sample of 29.

6.05 Application of improvements in appropriate national collective agreements in determining terms and conditions of work: company and divisional head office staffs

Manual

	Multi-establishment company		Division of multi	
	Number	Per cent	Number	Per cent
Always	27	26.5	12	41.4
Sometimes	26	25.5	5	17.2
Never	13	12.7	1	3.4
No response	36	35.3	11	37.9
	102	100.0	29	100.0

Non-manual

Always	21	20.6	7	24.1
Sometimes	32	31.4	6	20.7
Never	21	20.6	10	34.5
No response	28	27.5	6	20.7
	102	100.0	29	100.0

6.06a Pay systems and structures: company head office determined: manual employees

	Multi-establishment company		Division of multi	
	Number	Per cent	Number	Per cent
Pay system or structure applying to all or some divisions and establishments:				
all	34	33.3	11	37.9
some	20	19.6	4	13.8
none	48	47.1	12	41.4
If some or none attempts to co-ordinate pay settlements	42	61.8	7	43.7
Pay settlements reviewed annually	94	92.2	26	89.6
practice began:				
1979	2	2.1	1	3.4
1978	1	1.1	0	0.0
1977	1	1.1	0	0.0
1971–1976	13	13.8	6	20.6
1965–1970	18	19.2	2	6.9
1960–1964	4	4.2	2	6.9
1955–1959	4	4.2	1	3.4
1950–1954	0	0.0	4	15.4
before 1950	17	18.1	3	10.3
no response	34	36.2	7	24.1

6.06b Pay systems and structures: company head office determined:
non-manual employees

	Multi-establishment company		Division of multi	
	Number	Per cent	Number	Per cent
Pay system or structure applying to all or some divisions and establishments:				
all	49	48.0	13	44.8
some	23	22.5	4	13.8
none	30	29.5	10	34.5
If some or none attempts to co-ordinate pay settlements	36	67.9	8	57.1
Pay settlements reviewed annually as company head office policy	88	86.3	22	75.9
practice began:				
1979	2	2.3	1	4.5
1978	0	0.0	0	0.0
1977	3	3.4	0	0.0
1971−1976	11	12.5	6	27.3
1965−1970	25	28.4	1	4.5
1960−1964	5	5.7	3	13.5
1955−1959	2	2.3	1	4.5
1950−1954	1	1.1	4	18.3
before 1950	14	15.9	2	9.1
no response	25	28.4	4	18.3

6.06c   Pay systems and structures: divisionally determined

	Multi-establishment company		Division of multi	
	Number	Per cent	Number	Per cent
Pay system or structure applying to all or some establishments:				
all	14	48.3	18	62.1
some	15	51.7	2	6.9
none	0	0.0	8	27.6
If some or none attempts to co-ordinate pay settlements	7	46.7	7	70.0
Pay settlements reviewed annually as divisional policy	23	79.3	19	65.5
practice began:				
1979	0	0.0	1	5.3
1978	0	0.0	0	0.0
1977	0	0.0	0	0.0
1971–1976	6	26.1	4	21.0
1965–1970	4	17.5	2	10.5
1960–1964	1	4.3	3	15.8
1955–1959	1	4.3	0	0.0
1950–1954	2	8.7	4	21.0
before 1950	3	13.0	2	10.6
no response	6	26.1	3	15.8

6.07a   Policy on annual pay reviews: company head office

Pay

	Manual		Non-manual	
	Number	Per cent	Number	Per cent
Reviewed annually	94	92.2	88	86.3
Annual review practice began:				
1979	2	2.1	2	2.3
1978	1	1.1	0	0.0
1977	1	1.1	3	3.4
1971−1976	13	13.8	11	12.5
1965−1970	18	19.1	25	28.4
1960−1964	4	4.2	5	5.7
1955−1959	4	4.2	2	2.3
1950−1954	0	0.0	0	0.0
before 1950	17	18.1	14	15.9
no response	34	36.3	26	28.4

Conditions

	Manual		Non-manual	
Reviewed annually	34	33.3	28	27.5
Annual review practice began:				
1979	2	5.9	0	0.0
1978	1	2.9	1	3.6
1977	0	0.0	1	3.6
1971−1976	7	20.7	6	21.4
1965−1970	10	29.4	7	25.0
1960−1964	1	2.9	3	10.7
1955−1959	1	2.9	1	3.6
1950−1954	0	0.0	0	0.0
before 1950	3	8.8	1	3.6
no response	9	26.5	8	28.5

6.07b   Policy on annual pay reviews: division—head office policy

Pay

	Manual		Non-manual	
	Number	Per cent	Number	Per cent
Reviewed annually	26	89.7	22	75.9
Annual review practice began:				
1979	1	3.8	1	4.5
1978	0	0.0	0	0.0
1977	0	0.0	0	0.0
1971–1976	6	23.2	6	27.4
1965–1970	2	7.7	1	4.5
1960–1964	2	7.7	3	13.6
1955–1959	1	3.8	1	4.5
1950–1954	4	15.4	4	18.2
before 1950	3	11.5	2	9.1
no response	7	26.9	4	18.2

Conditions

	Manual		Non-manual	
Reviewed annually	12	41.4	14	48.3
Annual review practice began:				
1979	0	0.0	0	0.0
1978	0	0.0	0	0.0
1977	1	8.3	0	0.0
1971–1976	5	41.8	2	14.3
1965–1970	1	8.3	2	14.3
1960–1964	0	0.0	4	28.6
1955–1959	1	8.3	1	7.1
1950–1954	1	8.3	2	14.3
before 1950	2	16.7	1	7.1
no response	1	8.3	2	41.3

6.07c Policy on annual pay reviews: divisional level

Pay

	Manual		Non-manual	
	Number	Per cent	Number	Per cent
Reviewed annually	23	73.3	19	65.5
Annual review practice began:				
1979	0		1	
1978	0		0	
1977	0		0	
1971–1976	6		4	
1965–1970	4		2	
1960–1964	1		3	
1955–1959	1		0	
1950–1954	2		4	
before 1950	3		2	
no response	6		3	

Conditions

	Manual		Non-manual	
Reviewed annually	11	37.9	13	44.8
Annual review practice began:				
1979	0	0.0	0	0.0
1978	0	0.0	1	7.7
1977	0	0.0	0	0.0
1971–1976	5	45.4	3	23.1
1965–1970	2	18.2	1	7.7
1960–1964	1	9.1	1	7.7
1955–1959	0	0.0	0	0.0
1950–1954	1	9.1	2	15.4
before 1950	2	18.2	2	15.4
no response	0	0.0	3	23.1

7 The development of formality

The word 'formal', as employed, for example, by the Donovan Commission, is difficult to describe in a single phrase. Its *significance* is both institutional and procedural; its *expression* often, but not invariably, implies written rather than verbal formulation or acceptance of 'custom and practice'.

Participants in the survey understood 'formality' in all these senses. Some pointed to the establishment of joint consultative committees which had constitutions and met regularly, some to the appointment of employee relations specialists or of new management teams—all of them *institutional* changes—to describe the ways in which their approach had become more systematic; others referred to the adoption of grievance and disciplinary procedures arising out of Codes of Practice issued by ACAS—all of them *procedural* developments. A third group emphasised the *expression* of greater formality by referring to the drawing up of written works handbooks and agreements and the setting down of written rules to regulate pay, e.g. in job evaluation.

Almost 30 per cent of single establishment companies, 70 per cent of establishment of multis and 80 per cent or more of multi-establishment companies reported greater formality in their employee relations over the past ten years (7.1, 7.01). Some, of course, had adopted a formal approach to employee relations *before* that time, so that recent pressures for formalisation had affected them but little. For the most part, however, the companies—with exceptions which are discussed later—believed that they had moved some considerable way towards institutions and procedures which could be identified and examined by reference to written documents generally known and accepted by those concerned. While, as with pay systems and structures, no precise measurement of change is possible, there can be no doubt that this has been considerable. In what areas has it principally taken place, and why?

Works and staff handbooks

Works and staff handbooks embodying company information and rules of conduct to be observed by employees are probably the oldest form of documentation used in employee relations. In some industries, notably engineering, textiles and railways, these existed from the eighteenth century as a means of ensuring discipline in factory and para-military situations. They were never universal. At the end of the 1960s about two-thirds of engineering establishments had written works rules for manual workers, the incidence varying from 28 per cent in small factories employing fewer than 100 workers to 78 per cent in the largest employing over 1,000. The present survey suggests that there may have been a modest increase in the use of handbooks in the past decade, but little more than that. Almost 53 per cent of single-establishment companies reported that they had them for manual or staff employees or for both, 72 per cent of establishments of multis, 62 per cent of divisional headquarters and almost 70 per cent of multi-establishment company headquarters (7.5 and 7.06).

Historically, staff handbooks have probably made only a limited contribution to 'formalisation'. At the time of the 1969 engineering survey many were out of date and were evidently designed more to provide management with a fall-back position on non-negotiated terms and conditions of employment than to ensure an active base for regulating behaviour. When asked to suggest in what ways their approach to employee relations had become more systematic, respondents in the present survey seldom referred to works rules except, in a few instances, in the context of consolidation of existing rules into a single document.

Procedures

Written procedures for handling disputes and grievances and for laying down negotiating arrangements date at least from the middle of the last century. Most of these, as they had developed into the period following the last great war, had two principal characteristics — most were 'general' and most were industry-wide in character. Relatively few companies had internal procedures specially set down for their own purposes and relatively few had particular procedures for particular purposes, apparently

184

preferring to process all issues through the same channels. The 'internalising' and 'diversifying' of procedures became more widely accepted as desirable from the middle 1960s and received encouragement from the Donovan Commission and the Industrial Relations Act 1971 and the codes of practice which began to be issued on various subjects after that time.

The present survey shows individual grievance procedures to be almost universal in larger companies and their establishments, but somewhat less so in single establishment companies, and disciplinary procedures to be similar in number and distribution. Fewer companies had collective grievance procedures, but those dealing with lateness and absence were more common. In individual establishments of multis, where the effect of closed shops was greatest, union membership appeal procedures were almost universal, an interesting development of the past few years. It may be of interest that job evaluation, grading and employee appraisal procedures were as common as they appear to be, even for manual employees, affecting a considerable movement towards the application of these techniques (7.4 and 7.05).[1]

Documentation on individual contracts

Since July 1964 employers have been required by law to provide for individual employees a written 'statement of particulars' of the main terms of their employment. The object of the questions in the present inquiry was to obtain a view on whether or not companies now *exceed* this limited requirement by providing additional written statements on terms and conditions, or on pay and pay structure or by means of a confirmatory statement or checklist for new starters. In the case of headquarters divisions and establishments of multis, rather more than one half did so and 42 per cent of single establishment companies. Evidently employees are substantially better informed today than was once the case (7.3 and 7.04).

Codification and instructions for managers

In the past it has been rare for line and staff managers to be informed or instructed on company practice or policy in employee relations. The latter is discussed in a later chapter. Handbooks of practice for managers may be important not only for information, but also to enable consistency to prevail over the unit of management concerned. Fewer than

8 per cent of single establishment companies had such handbooks, but this increased to almost one-quarter in individual establishments and headquarters of multis and was highest at divisional level—over 40 per cent (7.2 and 7.02). Despite this change in some companies, an air of informality still prevails in many, indeed at least one-half of the survey companies, which either regard such a development as unnecessary or too inflexible and prefer to use more traditional methods or simply to deal with problems as they arise, leaving this to the good sense of managers themselves (7.03).

Extent of and reasons for greater formalisation

Some evidence of greater formalisation exists in all but 20 per cent of companies in the survey. In some, however, this has gone substantially further than in others. A few, particularly smaller companies, remain, it seems, substantially untouched and have, on the evidence they provided for us, hardly felt any pressures to which they felt compelled to accede. Of the 50 single establishment companies which fell into this category 32 (or 64 per cent) employed fewer than 50 employees and the smallest 40 fewer than 100. Yet a further 36 companies of comparable size admitted that they had been affected by formalisation. Size appears, in itself, not to be a criterion but rather, perhaps, the sensitivity of employers to social situations around them, or their perceived organisational needs. Some, particularly larger companies, commented that recent developments encouraging formalisation had affected them little because they had already moved substantially in that direction before such pressures began. Others, including relatively small companies, noted that, as they had grown, formalisation had built up in line with other developments in the conduct of the business. Sometimes this was associated with the hiring of employee relations specialists. In other cases the development of trade unionism within the factory was noted as the most important factor[1] and, in the third group, improved communications were seen as having given rise to a situation which required greater formality through committee procedures and similar devices. Some management perceived that managerial procedures in themselves, directly unconcerned with employee relations, such as more systematic ways of handling production control, orders and supplies, might have indirect effects and require more formal employee relations responses. 'Better paperwork', said more than one company, led to a decline in informality; the more records were kept, the more likely that these would spread into labour matters.

---

1 The situation seems to be affected more by the *initial* growth and recognition of trade unions rather than by their existence in general, and to apply particularly to single establishment companies.

Many respondents, however, attributed increases in formalisation directly to recent legislation, and particularly to the Trade Union and Labour Relations Act 1974 and the Employment Protection Act 1975. 'We have followed the legislation'. The Health and Safety at Work Act had evidently impressed some companies and was also given as a reason. This emphasis on the effects of recent legislation is broadly in line with the replies given to another question asked on the perceived influence of a number of events on company employee relations stretching from the National Board for Prices and Incomes between 1965 and 1970 to the 1975 EPA. Almost all companies appeared to see the latter, together with the 1971 Industrial Relations Act, as the events which had primarily affected them. Can this be taken to mean that company memories are short and that the Prices and Incomes Board, the Commission of Industrial Relations and Donovan have been forgotten or that direct legislative requirements such as those pioneered by the Contracts of Employment Act 1963 and developed so extensively from 1971 onwards are the devices which have had the most impact? There may be truth in both contentions, but there remains no doubt that it is legislation, rather than persuasion, whether this be direct or indirect, which makes the greater impression on the situation. 'Ten years ago' said a number of companies, 'we were totally informal. Now we feel that we must document all our systems.'

Summary

1. A substantial proportion of single establishment companies and a preponderance of multis saw their employee relations as having become more formal, either institutionally, procedurally or in relation to the setting down of rules.

2. There seems to have been only a modest increase in the use of works or staff handbooks, but there remains some doubt whether such documents have ever made much contribution to 'formalisation'.

3. The setting down of formal procedures relating to grievances and discipline appears to have become an almost universal practice; collective grievance procedures are less often found, but there has been growth in the areas of lateness and absence, union membership appeals, and in job evaluation, grading and staff appraisal.

4. The 'statement of particulars' of the main terms of employment of individuals which has been required by law since 1964 has been expanded into supplementary statements in a substantial number of companies.

5. There has been little codification of rules, practices and policy in the form of handbooks for managers.

6. While size of company plays some part in the tendency of companies to become more formalised, the sensitivity of employers to social situations and perceived organisational needs may be more important. Pressures for formalisation are seen as having come from a number of sources, legislation being high on the list, but other factors being more technically concerned with employee relations practice or advice to more systematic management generally, or to the advent of trade unionism.

References

Armstrong, Peter and Goodman, John. 'Managerial and supervisory custom and practice', *Industrial Relations Journal*, Vol.10, No.3, Autumn 1979.

Brown, William. 'A consideration of custom and practice', *British Journal of Industrial Relations*, Vol.X, No.1, March 1972.

Evans, E.O. 'Works Rules in Engineering', *Industrial Relations Journal*, Vol.2, No.1, Spring 1971.

Flanders, Allan. *Industrial Relations: What is wrong with the system?* Faber and Faber, 1965.

Gill, Colin C. 'Industrial Relations in a Multi-Plant Organisation', *Industrial Relations Journal*, Vol.5, No.4, Winter 1974–75.

Goodman, J.F.B. et al. 'Rules in Industrial Relations Theory', *Industrial Relations Journal*, Vol.6, No.1, Spring 1975.

Lumley, Roger. 'A modified rules approach to workplace industrial relations', *Industrial Relations Journal*, Vol.10, No.4, Winter 1979–80.

McCarthy, W.E.J., Parker, P.A., Howes, W.R. and Lumb, A.L. *The Reform of Collective Bargaining at Plant and Company Level*, Manpower Papers No.5, Department of Employment, HMSO, 1971.

Maitland, Ian. 'Disorder in the British Workplace: The Limits of Consensus', *British Journal of Industrial Relations*, Vol.XVIII, November 1980.

Purcell, John and Earl, Michael J., 'Control Systems and Industrial Relations', *Industrial Relations Journal*, Vol.8, No.2, Summer 1977.

Zimmerman, D. 'The Practicalities of Rule Use', in Salaman and Thompson, *People and Organisations*, Longmans, 1973.
'The Practicalities of Rule Use', in Douglas, J.D. (ed.), *Understanding Everyday Life*, Routledge and Kegan Paul.

Tabulations

The development of formality

7.1 Companies reporting that their approach to employee relations had become more systematic during the past ten years

Type of company	All companies	ERs more systematic	
		Number	Per cent
Single establishment	156	45	28.8
Establishment of multi	54	38	70.4
Division of multi	29	24	82.7
Multi-establishment	102	81	79.4
	341	188	55.1

7.2 Employee relations policies

	Single establishment company		Individual establishment multi	
	Number	Per cent	Number	Per cent
Board involved in:				
setting down of ER policies	39	25.0	23	50.0
ER handbook for managers	12	7.7	13	24.1
Decision taken at higher level in company	—	—	12	22.2

189

7.3 Employee relations documentation issued

	Single establishment company		Individual establishment multi	
	Number	Per cent	Number	Per cent
Statement of employee relations policy	36	23.1	25	46.3
Checklist for new starters	66	42.3	32	59.3
Confirmatory statement for new starters	70	44.9	35	64.8
Written statement on pay system or structure	64	41.0	30	55.6
Written statement on terms and conditions	66	42.3	38	70.4
Safety policy statement	123	78.8	47	87.0
Equal opportunities statement	12	7.7	14	25.9

7.4 Written procedures in operation

	Single establishment		Individual establishment	
	Manual	Non-manual	Manual	Non-manual
	Per cent			
Individual grievance	69.2	58.3	85.2	77.8
Collective grievance	39.7	32.0	57.4	53.7
Discipline: dismissal	79.9	57.1	85.2	79.6
Lateness and absence	60.9	48.1	83.3	72.2
TU recognition	23.7	16.0	37.0	33.3
Union membership appeal	12.1	8.3	85.2	85.2
Job evaluation	21.1	16.0	38.9	48.1
Grading appeal	16.0	11.5	44.4	44.4
Employee appraisal	19.8	19.2	27.8	37.0

7.5 Works and staff handbooks

	No handbook		Manual workers only		Non-manual workers only		Manual and non-manual workers jointly	
	No.	Per cent	No.	Per cent	No.	Per cent	No.	Per cent
Single establishment companies*	74	47.4	13	8.3	3	1.9	61	39.1
Of which:								
issue to all			11	84.6	0	0.0	53	86.9
issue on request			2	15.4	3	100.0	8	13.1
				100.0		100.0		100.0
Individual establishment multis**	15	27.8	4	7.4	2	3.7	33	61.1
Of which:								
issue to all			4	100.0	1	50.0	31	93.9
issue on request			0	0.0	1	50.0	2	6.1
				100.0		100.0		100.0

*   N = 156
** N = 54

7.6a Written and unwritten advice to managers on employee relations practice: where trade unions are to any extent recognised

	Single establishment company		Individual establishment multi	
	Number	Per cent	Number	Per cent
Companies recognising	93	59.6	39	78.2
Issuing written advice on further recognition or present recognition	8	8.6	3	7.7
Giving unwritten advice on further recognition or present recognition	26	27.9	10	25.6

Giving written advice or instruction on:	Manual	Non-manual	Manual	Non-manual
		Per cent		
facilities for trade unions	19.3	12.9	30.8	23.1
disclosure of information for collective bargaining	4.3	4.3	10.3	7.7
individual and collective grievance handling	53.8	39.8	74.3	66.7
handling of discipline	58.0	41.9	82.0	74.4
implementation of holiday arrangements	61.3	51.6	79.5	76.9
sick pay implementation	38.7	39.8	64.1	64.1
recruitment	20.4	16.1	43.6	41.0
selection	18.3	15.0	33.3	28.0
transfer	15.0	12.9	28.2	30.8

7.6b Written and unwritten advice to managers on employee relations practice: where trade unions are not recognised

	Single establishment company		Individual establishment multi	
	Number	Per cent	Number	Per cent
Companies not recognising	63	40.4	15	21.8
Issuing written advice on attitudes to or action on recognition	2	3.2	0	0.0
Giving unwritten advice on attitudes to or action on recognition	15	23.8	5	33.3
Giving written advice or instruction on:	Manual	Non-manual	Manual	Non-manual
		Per cent		
individual and collective grievance handling	15.9	15.9	46.7	46.7
handling of discipline	17.5	17.5	46.7	46.7
implementation of holiday arrangements	39.7	39.7	73.3	73.3
sick pay implementation	30.1	34.9	60.0	53.3
recruitment	7.9	6.3	6.7	13.3
selection	1.6	1.6	0.0	6.7
transfer	1.6	0.0	6.7	6.7

7.01   Companies reporting that their approach to employee relations had become more systematic during the past ten years

Type of company	All companies	ERs more systematic Number	Per cent
Single establishment	156	45	28.8
Establishment of multi	54	38	70.4
Division of multi	29	24	82.7
Multi establishment	102	81	79.4
	341	188	55.1

7.02 Formal employee relations policies

	Multi-establishment company		Division of multi	
	Number	Per cent	Number	Per cent
Board involved in:				
setting down of ER policies	51	50.0	11	37.9
ER handbooks for managers	24	23.5	12	41.4
Decision on policy or handbook taken:				
1979	6	10.5	4	23.5
1978	1	1.7	2	11.8
1977	3	5.3	2	11.8
1971−1976	16	28.1	3	17.6
1965−1970	7	12.3	1	5.9
1960−1964	0	0.0	0	0.0
1955−1959	0	0.0	0	0.0
1950−1954	0	0.0	0	0.0
before 1950	3	5.3	0	0.0
no response	21	36.8	5	29.4
	57	100.0	17	100.0
Intention of policy and handbook to provide:				
statement of principles	45	78.9	10	58.8
guide in making decisions	21	36.8	8	47.0
statement of rules	22	38.6	12	70.6
copies of collective agreements	18	31.6	7	41.2
Reason for issue of policy and handbook:				
to raise level of conduct of ERs	36	63.1	11	64.7
to obtain greater consistency	41	71.9	12	70.6
pressure of legislation	24	42.1	6	35.3
pressure from organised labour	8	14.0	1	5.9
to avoid TU organisation	2	3.5	1	5.9
to follow up-to-date practice	37	64.9	10	58.8
need for participation	29	50.9	0	0.0
advice by consultants	6	10.5	0	0.0
Documents reviewed and updated	41	71.9	11	64.7

7.03 No formal employee relations policies or handbooks

	Multi-establishment company		Division of multi	
	Number	Per cent	Number	Per cent
Once existed; now disused	0	0.0	2	6.9
Reasons for absence:				
not thought necessary	23	51.1	6	50.0
prefer flexibility	27	60.0	6	50.0
ER too decentralised	9	20.0	3	25.0
policy changed on reorganisation or take-over	1	2.2	3	25.0
All companies and divisions N = 45			12	
In absence of documented policies:				
use traditional procedures	34	75.5	6	50.0
deal with problems as they arise	35	77.8	8	66.7
leave to good sense of managers	26	57.8	4	33.3
by informal advice to managers	32	71.1	8	66.7
by using outside advice	20	44.4	5	41.7
by consultation and communication with employees	34	75.5	8	66.7

7.04 Employee relations documentation issued

	Multi-establishment company		Division of multi	
	Number	Per cent	Number	Per cent
Statement of employee relations policy	13	32.4	10	34.5
Checklist for new starters	47	46.1	11	37.9
Confirmatory statement for new starters	52	51.0	16	55.2
Written statement on pay system or structure	55	53.9	18	62.1
Written statement on terms and conditions	57	55.9	17	58.6
Safety policy statement	87	87.3	20	89.7
Equal opportunities statement	36	35.3	4	13.8

7.05 Written procedures in operation: company and divisional practice at establishments

	Multi-establishment company		Division of multi	
	Manual	Non-manual	Manual	Non-manual
	Per cent			
Individual grievance	90.2	88.3	82.7	79.3
Collective grievance	74.5	70.0	72.4	69.0
Discipline: dismissal	90.2	88.2	86.2	82.8
Lateness and absence	79.4	74.5	65.5	58.6
TU recognition	38.2	36.3	24.1	20.7
Union membership appeal	15.7	14.7	13.8	13.8
Job evaluation	46.1	53.9	31.0	37.9
Grading appeal	44.1	51.0	34.5	37.9
Employee appraisal	26.5	55.9	34.5	65.5

7.06 Works and staff handbooks: head office employees

	No handbook		Manual workers only		Non-manual workers only		Manual and non-manual workers jointly	
	No.	Per cent	No.	Per cent	No.	Per cent	No.	Per cent
Company HO	31	30.4	6	5.9	7	6.9	55	53.9
Of which:								
issue to all			4	66.7	7	100.0	46	83.6
issue on request			2	33.3	0	0.0	9	16.4
				100.0		100.0		100.0
Divisional HO		37.9	1	3.4	3	10.3	14	48.3
Of which:								
issue to all			1	100.0	3	100.0	12	85.7
issue on request			0	0.0	0	0.0	2	14.3
				100.0		100.0		100.0

7.07a Written and unwritten advice to managers on employee relations practice from company or divisional head office: where trade unions are to any extent recognised

	Multi-establishment company		Division of multi	
	Number	Per cent	Number	Per cent
Company or division recognising	90	88.2	24	82.8
Issuing written advice on further recognition or present recognition	30	33.3 Parent company	3	12.5
		Division	2	8.3
Giving unwritten advice on further recognition or present recognition	33	36.7 Parent company	2	8.3
		Division	11	45.8
Parent company giving written advice or instruction on:	Manual	Non-manual	Manual	Non-manual
		Per cent		
facilities for trade unions	41.2	31.4	8.3	4.2
disclosure of information for collective bargaining	26.5	20.6	12.5	12.5
individual and collective grievance handling	58.8	54.9	20.8	20.8
handling of discipline	57.8	54.9	29.2	29.2
implementation of holiday arrangements	56.8	52.9	41.7	41.7
sick pay implementation	58.8	59.8	29.2	33.3
recruitment	39.2	34.3	12.5	16.7
selection	29.5	31.4	16.7	20.8
transfer	39.2	38.2	16.7	25.0

7.07b Written and unwritten advice to managers on employee relations practice from company or divisional head office: where trade unions are not recognised

	Multi-establishment company		Division of multi	
	Number	Per cent	Number	Per cent
Company or division recognising	12	11.8	5	17.2
Issuing written advice on attitudes to or action on recognition	2	16.7 Parent company	1	20.0
		Division	1	20.0
Giving unwritten advice on attitudes to or action on recognition	5	41.7 Parent company	2	40.0
		Division	1	20.0

Parent company giving written advice or instruction on:	Manual	Non-manual	Manual	Non-manual
		Per cent		
individual and collective grievance handling	41.7	41.7	80.0	80.0
handling of discipline	50.0	50.0	80.0	80.0
implementation of holiday arrangements	66.7	66.7	80.0	80.0
sick pay implementation	75.0	66.7	60.0	60.0
recruitment	25.0	25.0	60.0	60.0
selection	8.3	8.3	60.0	60.0
transfer	25.0	25.0	60.0	60.0

8 Management style in employee relations

The background

The style in which a company approaches its employee relations activities is related to policy and to its philosophy of management; in some cases style, policy and philosophy may be entirely congruent; but this is not necessarily so. 'Style' may, indeed, convey more than policy and only partially reflect philosophy. It may represent general attitudes which, although less tangible, are nevertheless well understood to be the hallmark of each particular organisation. Sometimes it may go further and signify 'flair'.

Many style characteristics are attributed to employee relations in British industry. The 'cult' of informality already referred to would be widely accepted as one and preference for workplace settlement another. Both these have been discussed elsewhere in this study. It is also frequently contended that managements are parochial, if not smug, in their reluctance to seek advice, and that an obsession with activity commonly prevails over problem solving approaches which are considered (pejoratively) to be 'academic'. Some observers have labelled British management as 'reactive', i.e. as responding only to pressures or force of circumstance, and by implication have suggested that it ought to adopt a style of looking ahead, i.e. a style which is more 'proactive'. This chapter summarises how companies in the survey have characterised themselves in some of these respects.

External information and advice

All but a handful of companies (rather more than 8 per cent) claimed that they regularly sought information or advice (8.1 and 8.02a and b), and did so from a wide range of sources on a variety of matters of relevance to employee relations. The source most commonly used was the employers' association (or associations) to which the company belonged, especially where pay settlements were concerned. Here contact was high in all four types of company; at divisional level hardly any respondent said that it did not take place. But a considerable amount of information and advice was also, it was claimed, obtained from the CBI itself and from the Department of Employment and the Advisory, Conciliation and Arbitration Service, especially on employment law where solicitors featured prominently. Chambers of Commerce appear as a minor source and also outside consultants and retained advisers, but training boards appear to have established themselves as of some importance in such matters as health and safety and employee involvement. Remarkably little difference appeared in the pattern of usage as between single establishment companies, establishment of multis, divisions and headquarters of multis. Association of establishments into 'combines' has clearly not made them so dependent on parent companies as to inhibit the use of preferred outside sources of information and advice. The style, as noted elsewhere, is for such establishments to behave as nearly as possible as single establishment companies.

Publications received and consulted clearly favour the practical. At establishment level there was substantially no use at all for 'learned' journals (i.e. the *British Journal of Industrial Relations*, the *Industrial Relations Journal* and the *Labour Law Journal*); these were most likely to be received, although not necessarily consulted regularly, at divisions and headquarters. The general order of receipt and consultation varied little between the four types of company and ran in this order – *CBI Members Bulletin*,[1] Croner's *Reference Book for Employers, Management Today* (presumably the 'coffee table' publication of the set), employers' association circulars, *Industrial Relations Review and Report* and the *Department of Employment Gazette*, with *Personnel Management* occupying a higher place at division and headquarters levels (8.2, 8.03).

Aspects of style

There were no surprises in the replies of companies to questions which attempted to measure ways in which employee relations style had

1. This is sent to all members, although not all companies recorded the fact.

changed over the past decade. Companies, as already noted, thought of themselves as less autocratic and paternalistic and more participative and consultative. They believed in substantial numbers that they had become more 'formal' (see Chapter 7) and more 'negotiating' in their approaches to employee relations. Some admitted that a decade ago they had been 'hire and fire' companies but very few thought that this was still so. They identified in their activities a marked tendency towards *de*centralisation (see Chapter 6). Company attitudes to individualism and loyalty appeared to have changed little over the decade. Surprisingly, perhaps, in view of the statements sometimes made in connection with payment systems, there was some inclination to a development of 'incentive-mindedness', if not at division and headquarters level then certainly at establishments. Finally, a considerable proportion of companies believed that they were now less *re*active and more *pro*active (8.3 and 8.04).

This contention received support from a question which enquired into employee relations initiatives taken by companies in 1979 (8.4 and 8.05). Between 50 and 70 per cent of companies claimed that they had reviewed wage or salary payment systems or made other improvements.[1] It may be of interest that 'work restructuring for job satisfaction', frequently pressed in the 1970s as a means of improving the quality of working life, seems to have attracted little practical attention, while improved communication appears to have preoccupied divisions and headquarters more than establishments. Proactive attitudes are also reflected in Table 8.01.

Summary

1. Companies present themselves as open to information and advice on employee relations from a number of sources; they use these selectively, depending on the subject matter involved and make most generalised use of their own employers' organisations.

2. Publications received and consulted are those of a practical kind, 'learned journals' being rarely used.

3. Companies think of themselves as adopting a more participative and consultative style of management than was once the case; a considerable proportion consider that they are more 'proactive' than 'reactive'. In some other respects their attitudes may have changed very little. Recent developments such as 'work and other devices reckoned to increase job satisfaction' appear to have influenced them very little.

1 Compare this with the data on pay systems and structures, Chapter 6, p.154.

Tabulations

Management style in employee relations

8.1a External information and advice on employee relations: external information and advice sought

	Single establishment company		Individual establishment multi	
	Number	Per cent	Number	Per cent
Advice sought	137	97.9	51	94.4
Advice not sought	18	11.6	3	5.6
No response	1	0.6	–	–

8.1b External information and advice on employee relations: source
       of external information and advice

Subject	Health and safety		Employment law		Pay settlements		Employee involvement	
Source	S	I	S	I	S	I	S	I
	Per cent		Per cent		Per cent		Per cent	
CBI	23	20	29	31	26	24	26	35
Employers' assn.	36	37	42	31	50	39	26	17
Department of Employment	15	13	20	26	7	7	5	2
Chamber of Commerce	8	4	11	7	6	2	3	0
ACAS	6	7	19	31	10	15	8	15
Solicitors	5	9	32	37	2	2	1	0
Accountants	1	0	2	4	3	0	2	2
ITB	17	30	5	9	3	2	13	17
Consultants	3	7	3	6	3	9	5	6
Retained adviser	8	7	4	11	2	6	4	6
Average	12	13	17	19	11	11	9	10
Parent company	–	18	–	13	–	15	–	20
Division of parent company	–	2	–	4	–	4	–	4

S = Single establishment company
I = Individual establishment of a multi-establishment company

8.2 Publications received and consulted regularly

	Single establishment company		Individual establishment multi	
	Receive	Consult regularly	Receive	Consult regularly
	Per cent	Per cent	Per cent	Per cent
CBI Members Bulletin	89.7	61.5	88.9	53.7
Croner's Reference Book	55.8	49.4	61.1	50.0
Management Today	42.9	21.8	60.3	29.7
Empl. Association Circular	29.5	26.3	31.5	22.2
Ind. Relations Review and Report	21.8	16.7	40.7	22.2
Ind. Relations Law Reports	13.5	9.0	24.1	14.8
DE Gazette	12.8	8.3	29.6	20.4
Personnel Management	12.2	0.6	33.3	18.5
Croner's Empl. Digest	11.5	0.6	11.1	3.7
Incomes Data Services R & B	9.6	7.7	37.1	27.8
Company Secretary Review	9.0	6.4	14.9	9.3
Industrial Relations Journal	2.6	1.3	5.6	3.7
British Journal of Ind. Rels.	0.6	1.3	0.0	0.0
Labour Law Journal	0.6	0.6	0.0	0.0
Average	21.4	14.8	30.2	28.2

8.3 Company style in employee relations

Style	Single establishment company		Individual establishment multi	
	Today	In the past	Today	In the past
	Per cent	Per cent	Per cent	Per cent
Paternalistic	48.7	64.1	22.2	38.9
Autocratic	6.4	31.4	1.9	33.3
Participative	74.4	43.6	74.1	42.6
Teamwork	39.7	28.3	50.0	18.5
Individualistic	60.9	58.9	42.6	20.4
Formal	25.0	5.7	40.7	35.2
Informal	60.9	74.4	29.6	25.9
Centralised	13.5	18.0	9.3	7.6
Decentralised	52.5	43.5	63.0	18.6
Loyalistic	64.1	66.0	63.0	14.8
Functional	50.0	41.7	57.4	16.7
Incentive-minded	48.7	40.4	35.2	11.2
Employee-oriented	75.4	67.3	64.8	18.5
Hire and fire	2.6	6.4	1.9	9.4
Negotiating	41.1	32.7	35.2	22.2
Consultative	68.8	43.6	63.0	35.2
Reactive	20.5	37.1	11.1	18.5
Proactive	62.8	41.0	62.9	22.2

8.4 Employee relations initiatives in 1979

	Single establishment company		Individual establishment multi	
	Number	Per cent	Number	Per cent
Review or restructuring of wage payment system	97	62.2	40	74.1
Review or restructuring of salary payment system	84	53.8	43	79.6
Improved financial incentives	87	55.8	29	53.7
Improved working conditions	112	71.8	44	81.5
Work restructuring for job satisfaction	57	36.5	16	29.6
Improved communications	42	26.9	20	37.0

8.01 Considerations in locating and commissioning new factory or depot

Location	Single establishment company	Individual establishment company	Multi-establishment company	Division of multi
	Total percentages first three preferences			
Communication road and rail	57.7	57.4	47.1	41.3
TU organisation in area	8.3	11.1	4.9	6.9
TU officials in area	10.9	14.9	4.9	6.0
Relative development costs	N/A	N/A	43.1	48.2
Unemployment in area	10.9	11.2	10.7	17.2
Availability of skilled labour	52.6	53.7	51.9	41.3
Support services or trades	23.7	35.2	14.8	13.7
Preference town site	10.9	1.9	6.8	3.4
Preference— rural site	10.3	3.7	5.9	3.4
Available premises	23.7	24.1	16.7	20.7
Government financial assistance	30.1	20.5	24.5	31.0
Pay structure				
Before production begins	86.5	94.4	83.3	93.1
After production begins	10.3	0.0	8.8	6.9
Grievance procedures				
Before production begins	76.3	85.2	78.4	79.3
After production begins	18.6	7.4	13.7	20.7

8.02a   External information and advice on employee relations: external information and advice sought

	Multi-establishment companies		Divisions of multis	
	Number	Per cent	Number	Per cent
Advice sought	95	93.1	28	96.6
Advice not sought	7	6.9	1	3.4
No response	0	0.0	0	0.0

8.02b   External information and advice on employee relations: source of external information and advice

Subject Source	Health and safety		Employment law		Pay settlements		Employee involvement	
	HQ	Div.	HQ	Div.	HQ	Div.	HQ	Div.
	Per cent		Per cent		Per cent		Per cent	
CBI	20	14	33	24	32	24	34	24
Employers' assn.	33	38	38	45	47	58	17	21
Department of Employment	21	10	43	31	17	7	10	7
Chamber of Commerce	4	3	6	3	3	3	3	3
ACAS	4	0	40	38	26	14	17	7
Solicitors	2	3	40	28	2	0	2	0
Accountants	1	0	4	0	1	3	1	0
ITB	25	21	6	7	4	0	15	17
Consultants	5	3	7	3	9	7	11	14
Retained adviser	6	7	9	7	3	10	6	7
Average	12	10	23	15	14	13	11	9
Parent company	–	17	–	17	–	28	–	24

8.03 Publications received and consulted regularly

	Multi-establishment company		Division of multi	
	Receive	Consult regularly	Receive	Consult regularly
	Per cent	Per cent	Per cent	Per cent
CBI Members Bulletin	92.1	64.7	72.4	44.8
Croner's Reference Book	71.5	62.7	65.5	51.7
Management Today	67.6	24.5	58.6	27.6
Empl. Assn. Circular	42.2	37.3	68.9	51.7
Ind. Relations Review & Report	67.5	60.8	58.6	48.3
Ind. Relations Law Reports	47.1	30.4	30.1	20.7
DE Gazette	56.9	39.3	41.4	34.5
Personnel Management	62.7	40.2	58.6	41.4
Croner's Empl. Digest	19.6	17.7	20.7	73.8
Incomes Data Services R & B	58.9	54.0	48.3	48.3
Company Secretary Review	25.5	16.7	10.3	0.0
Industrial Relations Journal	23.5	8.8	10.3	10.3
British Journal of Ind. Relations	13.7	3.9	6.9	6.9
Labour Law Journal	2.9	2.9	0.0	0.0
Average	46.5	33.3	39.3	28.5

8.04 Company style in employee relations

Style	Multi-establishment company		Division of multi	
	Today	In the past	Today	In the past
	Per cent	Per cent	Per cent	Per cent
Paternalistic	26.4	71.5	27.5	68.9
Autocratic	6.9	48.1	13.8	55.2
Participative	69.6	22.6	72.4	24.1
Teamwork	53.0	26.5	48.3	24.1
Individualistic	43.1	56.8	67.0	65.5
Formal	54.1	22.6	65.5	20.6
Informal	31.4	49.0	20.6	68.9
Centralised	29.4	46.0	17.2	27.6
Decentralised	46.1	21.6	75.9	51.7
Loyalistic	54.7	62.7	62.1	75.7
Functional	50.0	38.2	62.0	37.9
Incentive-minded	40.2	39.2	44.8	41.5
Employee-oriented	56.9	58.8	72.4	68.7
Hire and fire	6.9	8.8	3.4	10.3
Negotiating	48.1	26.5	44.8	31.0
Consultative	64.7	30.4	79.3	27.6
Reactive	11.7	34.3	24.1	48.3
Proactive	58.9	39.3	56.6	31.0

8.05 Employee relations initiatives in 1979

	Multi-establishment company		Division of multi	
	Number	Per cent	Number	Per cent
Review or restructuring of wage payment system	51	50.0	20	69.0
Review or restructuring of salary payment system	62	60.8	19	65.5
Improved financial incentives	55	53.9	12	41.4
Improved working conditions	15	63.7	19	63.5
Work restructuring for job satisfaction	28	27.5	9	31.0
Improved communications	54	52.9	20	69.0

9 Policy and decision making

The background

Businessmen are reputed to dislike the word 'policy' because of its supposed connection with government and political discussion. In practice no such connotation need to be read into it. 'Policy' may simply be thought of as a guide to making decisions or, more elaborately 'a list or system of principles by appeal to which we can answer the question what to do in this or that set of circumstances'. This notion seems to be as readily applied to management as to any other sphere of activity. A marketing policy, for example, may be thought of as a set of rules and priorities on what to produce and sell and to whom, the means to be applied in doing so and the prices to be charged, together with indications as to how contingencies might be met and the rules of conduct revised.

Employee relations appears to be as good a candidate for this kind of treatment as any other. Indeed, it would be difficult to imagine any enterprise employing labour which can in practice avoid such a device. Decisions about recruitment, pay, discipline, dismissal and other personnel matters have to be taken according to some pattern or purpose. The question is not, however, whether or not such decisions, taken together, constitute a *de facto* policy, but whether such a *de facto* approach is sufficient. If it is not, what, in employee relations terms constitutes an *explicit* policy and who ought properly to be involved in creating it and by what means?

In principle, the argument for movement from *de facto* to explicit policies is a strong one. Streams of decisions made at various levels from foreman to managing director may generate a series of outcomes which are inconsistent one with another; discipline, for example, may be harsher in one shop than another, pay may be less generous in some parts of the enterprise than in others, with consequent disputes or complaint about unfairness. Merely to deal with such grievances as they arise may not be enough without some guidance to managers on how particular kinds of subject matter ought to be handled. Some concession to complete managerial flexibility becomes essential. Such a view became standard in publicly sponsored advice to managements in the 1970s.

But how far ought such regulation to go? Would it be advisable for private employers to develop rules and advices to cover *all* foreseeable contingencies (after the fashion of the Estacode of the Civil Service), or is it necessary to cover key areas of policy only? Are such rules and advices sufficient without the adoption of an overall philosophy of labour management understood by everyone and acting as the final touchstone and guide to action? If so, is this and other policy determination essentially, as the Donovan Commission suggested, a matter for management boards at the highest level in the company, or can it be left to employee relations specialists? If the latter is the proper course of action, how are specialists to apply policy when this appears to be in conflict with commercial realities, e.g. where 'no-redundancy', if this is part of such a policy, conflicts with a labour surplus arising from a drastic fall in demand?

The survey

From Chapter 4 it would be difficult to conclude that main boards of companies greatly concern themselves with policy making in any explicit sense. More of this is no doubt done where there are main board employee relations directors, but it seems evident enough that boards operate either by *de facto* methods or are, as already noted (p.103) often content to endorse decisions taken elsewhere or to become directly involved only when the situation is judged sufficiently serious to merit their attention. Although there has unquestionably been a movement, especially in large multi-establishment concerns, to emphasise the need for explicit policy making, this seems very likely to have been generated from below board level. It may, in fact, be regarded more as an administrative than an executive function. It is arguable that the executive character of British boards lays such heavy emphasis on the activity roles of directors that the taking of policy decisions in the classic sense, i.e. by open discussion about general propositions, is only rarely possible. Failing such discussion, the development of policy may lie with board committees or with employee relations specialists who have professional reasons for wishing to clarify behaviour and attitudes in order to encourage consistency in employee relations. Such specialists may submit such developments for board approval if they fit into the action frame of the boards themselves, but may think it wiser to retain others on an administrative level only.

It must be admitted that on the evidence of the survey alone some part of this view is no more than partially informed speculation.[1] Beyond the mere nuts and bolts aspects of policies, however, a high proportion of companies of all kinds were insistent that they had philosophies of employee relations—82 per cent of multis, 70 per cent of singles, 62 per cent of divisions and 52 per cent of establishments of multis (9.1; 9.01). A small number produced documents. These included Massey Ferguson whose approach to the matter has been discussed elsewhere.[2] Few documents were as comprehensive as those of Massey's; in some instances they were in the nature of 'statements of intent'. Most companies, both large and small, clearly preferred to avoid making such statements but thought nevertheless that they had overall approaches which were well understood in their organisations.

A list of the statements made by multi-establishment companies in response to our question about the philosophy of relationships adopted in their enterprises is given in Appendix 4. Broadly, these fell into six orientations: general philosophical, industrial relations, managerial/man management, manpower organisation, social and disciplinary. A few were difficult to categorise.

General philosophical orientations referred to 'respect for the dignity of man', to the encouragement of a 'participative, open environment', to 'rights and responsibilities' and 'fair and generous' treatment, to integrity and to the notion of 'the leader as the servant of those responsible to him'. *Industrial relations* orientations laid the emphasis differently: 'to observe good personnel practice', to 'keep within the law and deal justly with grievances and problems', to 'accept bargaining and staff participation'.

Where *management/man management* formed the basis of the philosophy of employee relations, stress was placed on the responsibility of managers for their staff, the need to accept rules and guidance, or to operate autonomously, the necessity for 'positive, clear-cut leadership'

---

1 It is, however, not out of line with a study of boards by Christopher Brooks (1979) in which directors tended to emphasise that their boards *generated* policy, drawing on its own expertise rather than *ratifying* decisions arrived at elsewhere, *deciding* whether to adopt policies formulated elsewhere, or *evaluating* between options provided for them.

2 Harry Hebden, Personnel Director of M-F, in Cuthbert and Hawkins (eds.), *Company Industrial Relations Policies*, Longman, 1973.

216

and upon employee relations roles—'senior management takes responsibility for industrial relations in conjunction with the group's personnel manager'. This bore some resemblance to companies who emphasised *manpower organisation* who addressed themselves, however, more to employees — 'that employees are one of the company's most important assets and have to be treated as such to secure the company's future' and, said another company, 'to pay them accordingly'. Others spoke of the availability of necessary 'human resources', the use of 'the minimum number of people commensurate with the efficient running of the business', the rewarding of skill, the provision of careers, and like matters.

Greater *social* emphasis appeared in some company statements. That 'all employees are treated the same', that there should be 'continuity of employment, person to person contact, fair treatment', 'a firm management understanding and objective, reconciled with employee aims' or, with more organisational emphasis, 'to keep units small and involve staff'. More *disciplinary* approaches were less common: 'treat them fairly, pay them well and don't stand any nonsense', 'know all your employees —don't let trouble makers start—get rid of them at any price'.

Policy and decision making

Board composition and habits apart, it may be that one reason for the avoidance of a more explicit approach to policy which seems to characterise British industry where employee relations are concerned is the desire by boards to retain both flexibility for subordinates and its own freedom to intervene in particular situations as it feels necessary. In some sense policy implies both regulation and delegation. It prescribes what action is required and authorises those responsible at the levels affected to behave accordingly. Delegation, some observers have noted, is not a popular system of decision making among managers, who prefer to decide for themselves after prior consultation.[1] Such a preference is hardly consonant with any policy except the most general and procedural.

The present survey confirms the continuing willingness of companies to accept the principle of prior consultation with their employees (Chapter 5). A similar approach is reflected in multi-establishment company practice towards subsidiary companies, divisions and establishments (9.02). Few such divisions or establishments were regarded as 'wholly independent' or 'wholly subordinate'. Mostly, and in almost equal numbers, they were reported as being 'restricted in what they could do without head office approval' or 'subject to periodic advice and direction'. 'Continuous advice and direction' was also rare. Many companies,

1   See, for example, Frank Heller, *Managerial Decision Making,* Tavistock, 1971.

through employee relations committees, regular meetings of directors of subsidiaries or of employee relations specialists (9.03) are evidently, through the use of such meetings, employing prior consultation with their own subordinates as an important element in the employee relations scene. Indeed, it seems that prior consultation may itself be elevated into a policy, leaving detailed decisions to evolve from lower levels and, where it seems necessary, remain subject to confirmation by the main board.

Our 50 company inquiry would, in general, confirm this view of the situation which is also compatible with the finding that 'formalisation' in employee relations (see Chapter 7) leads only very infrequently to consolidation of documents into comprehensive handbooks for the guidance of managers. Written advice, widely issued on some subjects, probably appeared as a response to particular needs, some arising from operational considerations and others from the requirements or advice contained in law or codes of practice. It continues to be regarded in that light and not as part of some overall framework of policy emanating from higher or main board level (9.05). It is interesting to note that in this connection the presence or absence of trade unions is hardly ever a deciding factor (9.05b).

It thus seems that British companies continue to prefer decisions after prior consultation and the evolution of discrete documentation and guidance to more bureaucratic methods of determining and modifying employee relations policy both at main board level and elsewhere. They also seem to use employee relations specialists as an important element in this process. How the philosophy of relationships which many companies can identify emerges from this process, or how the process shapes the philosophy, we cannot say. Nor would we feel, from the evidence of the survey, able to state with any certainty whether, in adopting a 'prior consultation' approach to policy boards were deliberately distancing themselves from employee relations or whether 'unconcern' or 'control by stealth' were elements in the situation. If pressed, we would probably be inclined to argue that neither was necessarily the case. It may be simpler and more apposite to point, not to moral or strategic considerations, but simply to the history of employee relations. Traditionally the handling of such matters has been regarded as peacemaking, the creation of procedures which are both 'treaties of peace and devices for avoiding war'.[1] Such an approach requires neither initiatives nor policies, but only a willingness to listen and discuss when necessary and, above all, to allow freedom for lower levels of management to settle differences as near the shop floor as possible, leaving only the most intractable issues, or those involving issues of principle to rise to board

---

1. A.I. Marsh, *Dispute Procedures in British Industry,* Royal Commission on Trade Unions and Employers' Associations, Research Papers 2 (Part 1), 1966, vii.

level. Boards are only acting as they have been accustomed to act. Whether the time has now come for a change is a different matter.

Summary

British manufacturing company boards, almost regardless of company size, tend to accept the notion that it is proper for them to have a general philosophy which enshrines their style of management, but continue to prefer an 'action' frame for their employee relations to the production of policies which might serve as a guide to day-to-day decision making both for themselves and for other levels of management. In doing so they appear to be following a long established tradition of *ad hoc* grievance settlement and the making of decisions after prior consultation and to find these preferable to more bureaucratic methods of determining and modifying employee relations policy at main board level and elsewhere in their companies.

References

Brewster, C.J., Gill, G.C. and Richbell, S. 'Industrial Relations Policy: A Framework for Analysis' in Thurley K.E. and Wood, S. (eds.), *Management Strategy and Industrial Relations,* (forthcoming).

Brooks, Christopher. *Boards of Directors in British Industry*, Department of Employment Research Paper No.7, August 1979.

Commission on Industrial Relations. *The Role of Management in Industrial Relations*, Report No.34, 1973.

Cuthbert, N.H. and Hawkins, K. *Company Industrial Relations Policies*, Longman, 1973.
and Whitaker, A., 'Industrial Relations: a matter of policy', *Personnel Management,* August 1976.

Gill, C.G. and Concannon, H.M.G., 'Developing an Explanatory Frame-'Industrial Relations: a matter of policy', *Personnel Management,* August 1976.

Gill, C.G. and Concannon, H.M.G. 'Developing and Explanatory Framework for Industrial Relations within the Firm', *Industrial Relations Journal*, Vol.7, No.3, Winter 1976/77.

Goodman, J.F.B. et al. 'Rules in Industrial Relations Theory', *Industrial Relations Journal*, Vol.6, No.1, Spring 1975.

McCarthy, W.E.J. and Ellis, N.D. *Management by Agreement*, Hutchinson, 1973.

Marsh, Arthur 'Company Policy', in C. Northcote Parkinson (ed.),

Industrial Disruption, Leviathan, 1973.

Ministry of Labour and National Service *Positive Employment Policies*, HMSO, 1958.

Pigors, F. and P. 'Who Should Make Personnel Policies?' *Personnel*, November 1950.

Poole, Michael, 'Managerial Strategies and Industrial Relations' in Poole, Michael and Mansfield, Roger (eds.), *Managerial Roles and Industrial Relations*, Gower, 1980.

Purcell, John. and Earl, Michael J. 'Control Systems and Industrial Relations', *Industrial Relations Journal*, Vol.8, No.2, Summer 1977.

Purcell, John. 'Applying Control Systems to Industrial Relations', *Journal of the Operational Research Society*, Vol.30, 1979.
'The Lessons of the CIR's attempts to reform workplace relations', *Industrial Relations Journal*, Vol.10, No.2, Summer 1979.
'A Strategy for Management Control in Industrial Relations', in Purcell, John and Smith, Robin (eds.), *The Control of Work*, Macmillan, 1979.

Smith, Robin, 'Work Control and Managerial Prerogative in Industrial Organisations'; paper to SSRC Seminar on *The Management Function in Industrial Relations*, December 1977.
'The Maximisation of Control in Industrial Relations Systems', in Purcell, John and Smith, Robin (eds), *The Control of Work*, Macmillan, 1979.

Tabulations

Policy and decision making

9.1   Has a philosophy of employee relations

	Single establishment company		Individual establishment multi	
	Number	Per cent	Number	Per cent
	110	70.5	28	51.9

9.2a Written and unwritten advice to managers on employee relations practice: where trade unions are to any extent recognised

	Single establishment company		Individual establishment multi	
	Number	Per cent	Number	Per cent
Companies recognising	93	59.6	39	78.2
Issuing written advice on further recognition or present recognition	8	8.6	3	7.7
Giving unwritten advice on further recognition or present recognition	26	27.9	10	25.6
Giving written advice or instruction on:	Manual	Non-manual	Manual	Non-manual
		Per cent		
facilities for trade unions	19.3	12.9	30.8	23.1
disclosure of information for collective bargaining	4.3	4.3	10.3	7.7
individual and collective grievance handling	53.8	39.8	74.3	66.7
handling of discipline	58.0	41.9	82.0	74.4
implementation of holiday arrangements	61.3	51.6	79.5	76.9
sick pay implementation	38.7	39.8	64.1	64.1
recruitment	20.4	16.1	43.6	41.0
selection	18.3	15.0	33.3	28.0
transfer	15.0	12.9	28.2	30.8

9.2b Written and unwritten advice to managers on employee relations practice: where trade unions are not recognised

	Single establishment company		Individual establishment multi	
	Number	Per cent	Number	Per cent
Companies not recognising	63	40.4	15	21.8
Issuing written advice on attitudes to or action on recognition	2	3.2	0	0.0
Giving unwritten advice on attitudes to or action on recognition	15	23.8	5	33.3

Giving written advice or instruction on:	Manual	Non-manual	Manual	Non-manual
		Per cent		
individual and collective grievance handling	15.9	15.9	46.7	46.7
handling of discipline	17.5	17.5	46.7	46.7
implementation of holiday arrangement	39.7	39.7	73.3	73.3
sick pay implementation	30.1	34.9	60.0	53.3
recruitment	7.9	6.3	6.7	13.3
selection	1.6	1.6	0.0	6.7
transfer	1.6	0.0	6.7	6.7

9.01 Has a philosophy of employee relations

Multi-establishment company		Division of multi	
Number	Per cent	Number	Per cent
84	82.4	18	62.1

9.02 Company practice in respect of the independence of subsidiary companies, divisions and establishments

	Multi-establishment company		Division of multi	
	Number	Per cent	Number	Per cent
Subsidiary companies or divisions				
wholly independent	6	5.9	12	41.4
partly independent	53	52.0	12	41.4
mostly subordinate	18	17.6	1	3.4
wholly subordinate	9	8.8	2	6.9
not applicable	7	6.9	0	0.0
no response	9	8.8	2	6.9
	102	100.0	29	100.0
'Partly independent' means:				
periodic advice and direction only	22	41.5	10	83.3
continuous advice and direction	5	9.5	0	0.0
certain actions only without co. approval	22	41.5	2	16.7
no important action without co. approval	4	7.5	0	0.0
	53	100.0	12	100.0
Individual establishments*				
wholly independent	2	7.7	1	5.9
partly independent	10	38.5	7	41.2
mostly subordinate	10	38.5	6	35.3
wholly subordinate	4	15.3	3	17.6
	26	100.0	17	100.0
'Partly independent' means:				
periodic advice and direction only	6	60.0	3	42.8
continuous advice and direction	1	10.0	2	28.6
certain actions only without approval	3	30.0	2	28.6
	10	100.0	7	100.0

* In the case of multi-establishment companies where establishments report directly to head office.

9.03 Hold periodic meetings of directors, managers and specialists on employee relations

	Multi-establishment company		Division of multi	
	Number	Per cent	Number	Per cent
All companies or divisions	102	100.0	29	100.0
Chairmen or MDs of subsidiary companies or divisions	30	29.4	4	13.8
Chief executives of organisations in divisions	–	–	(10)	(34.5)
ER directors or chief executives of subsidiaries	33	32.4	3	10.3
Senior ER staff of divisions	–	–	(10)	(34.5)
Companies or divisions holding meetings	40	39.2	6(13)	20.7(44.8)
of which hold:				
annually	3	7.5	1(1)	16.7(7.7)
half-yearly	6	15.0	1(2)	16.7(15.4)
quarterly	9	22.5	1(2)	16.7(15.4)
monthly	13	32.5	0(1)	0.0(7.7)
weekly	1	2.5	0(1)	0.0(7.7)
on request	8	20.0	3(6)	50.0(46.1)
	40	100.0	6(13)	100.0

9.04 Source of difficulty in co-ordinating employee relations decisions and activity

	Multi-establishment company		Division of multi	
	Number	Per cent	Number	Per cent
Disparity between main board structure and ER requirements	7	6.9	2	6.9
Differences between divisions and head office	19	18.6	2	6.9
Relations between trade unions at company level	22	21.6	NA	NA
Relations between trade unions below company level	23	22.5	4	13.8
Lower level management believes ERs too centralised	14	13.7	3	10.3
Head office believes ERs too centralised	8	7.8	1	3.4
Obtaining adequate ER staff	7	6.9	3	10.3

9.05a Written and unwritten advice to managers on employee relations practice from company or divisional head office: where trade unions are to any extent recognised

	Multi-establishment company		Division of multi	
	Number	Per cent	Number	Per cent
Company or division recognising	90	88.2	24	82.8
Issuing written advice on further recognition or present recognition	30	33.3 Parent company 3		12.5
		Division 2		8.3
Giving unwritten advice on further recognition or present recognition	33	36.7 Parent company 2		8.3
		Division 1		45.8

Parent company giving written advice or instruction on:	Manual	Non-manual	Manual	Non-manual
		Per cent		
facilities for trade unions	41.2	31.4	8.3	4.2
disclosure of information for collective bargaining	26.5	20.6	12.5	12.5
individual and collective grievance handling	58.8	54.9	20.8	20.8
handling of discipline	57.8	54.9	29.2	29.2
implementation of holiday arrangements	56.8	52.9	41.7	41.7
sick pay implementation	58.8	59.8	29.2	33.3
recruitment	39.2	34.3	12.5	16.7
selection	29.5	31.4	16.7	20.8
transfer	39.2	38.2	16.7	25.0

9.05b Written and unwritten advice to managers on employee relations practice from company or divisional head office: where trade unions are not recognised

	Multi-establishment company		Division of multi	
	Number	Per cent	Number	Per cent
Company or division recognising	12	11.8	5	17.2
Issuing written advice on attitudes to or action on recognition	2	16.7 Parent company Division	1 1	20.0 20.0
Giving unwritten advice on attitudes to or action on recognition	5	41.7 Parent company Division	2 1	40.0 20.0

Parent company giving written advice or instruction on:	Manual	Non-manual	Manual	Non-manual
		Per cent		
individual and collective grievance handling	41.7	41.7	80.0	80.0
handling of discipline	50.0	50.0	80.0	80.0
implementation of holiday arrangements	66.7	66.7	80.0	80.0
sick pay implementation	75.0	66.7	60.0	60.0
recruitment	25.0	25.0	60.0	60.0
selection	8.3	8.3	60.0	60.0
transfer	25.0	25.0	60.0	60.0

10 Summary and prospects

A decade is but a short time in the life of a system of industrial relations which has been at least a century and a half in the making. Yet there is much to be said for the view that the developments of the last ten years in Britain have been unique in that history. This is not because it has been unusual in that history for worker–management relations to be regarded as a source of industrial (and democratic) weakness and as a candidate for urgent reform. A series of Royal Commissions on the subject bear witness to the contrary. The last decade, and some years preceding it, have been unusual in that attention to employee relations has been unremitting, and that, for the first time in at least 100 years substantial legal changes have been made which have had bearing, not only on a wide range of factors in employment relationships, but also on managements. It is only during that period of time that *laissez-faire* has, even more for managers than trade unions, ceased to be the order of the day. In principle the change has been dramatic. Not so long ago, such incursions into 'voluntarism' would have been unthinkable and such attribution of responsibilities to management intolerable.

Managements have evidently not found it so. Some of the reasons emerge from this survey. In the first place, the changes required have been mainly procedural; in the second they have been compatible with the continuation of a great deal of variety in management style and organisation. Thirdly, they have probably brought from companies very little positive change in how those companies are organised. Despite the alarms and excursions of legislative reversals, of political retreats and advances and of unwelcome pressures from enthusiasts for industrial democracy, with tacit support from the European Community; despite the speed with which changes have taken place, the old system remains recognisable in the way in which companies seek to order their affairs. There has been no revolution. Some companies have hardly adjusted at all. Others have innovated more rapidly. All, it seems, have found it possible to cope with the situation by the use of committees and an admixture of personnel professionalism. These points may be worth further development in this summary since they are likely to form the background to any future attempts at public intervention in the employee relations field.

On the variety of situations to be found in different companies very little need to be said. Differences in size, product, ownership, organisation and style are evident enough. Trends are probably more important. British based companies, whether UK or foreign owned, feel themselves to be more consultative, participative, to be more involved in negotiation; they feel themselves to be less authoritarian and paternalistic. So much could have been anticipated. Their caution in handling their progress along such paths might also have been observed by anyone closely in touch with the industrial situation. 'Industrial democracy' in its more extended meanings or even in the narrower senses employed by the EEC or the Bullock Committee has impressed them but little. Firms have seen extensions of informal consultation, of more formal consultative committees and of communications exercises in their various forms as the obvious way forward in employer/employee relations in their enterprises.

Despite the growth of multi-establishment concerns in the past two decades as a result of mergers and acquisitions, the move to centralise employee relations in head offices, or even in divisions, has been limited. Although from the 1960s on they appear to have become more conscious of the need for orderly pay settlement and the necessity to devise pay systems and structures which will avoid 'drift' and competing claims and encourage productivity, there has been limited desire to organise bureaucratic arrangements from the centre. A great deal of work has, however, been put in on methods of co-ordinating claims and settlements by means which vary considerably from one company to another. The ideal of a management unit remains, however, the 'establishment'. For reasons which are evidently seen as good and sufficient, the ideal to which establishments seek to attain is not that of branch factory in a centralised conglomerate, but that of single establishment company, making, so far as possible its own decisions, and handling its labour force as best it may.

Specialist employee relations staff appear to have become important to UK manufacturing firms partly for their specific skills in job evaluation and other techniques, partly as co-ordinators and custodians of the development of policy-type approaches to problems and partly as advisers to line management. In almost all companies, it is the production management, in one form or another, which continues to dominate the employee relations scene in a day-to-day sense. The build up of specialists, so marked in numbers since the middle 1960s, has not been accepted as a device to replace direct relationships between employer and employed. While boards of directors have in many cases been adapted to meet the developing emphasis on personnel affairs there is no evidence that this has greatly altered their style of operation or their composition. Boards appear to concern themselves with issues of substance rather than of policy *per se*. While, in larger enterprises especially, serious attention is paid to employee relations, specialist board directors, where they have been appointed, are expected to row in for the *company* rather than for employee relations alone. Many companies prefer to allow overall responsibility to remain with non-specialists at board level, supported by specialist executives, where, paradoxically, their influence may be greater. Specialists with line experience are, however, beginning to filter through to the highest level of companies in other guises, as production or managing directors, for example.

Relatively few companies have taken the increasing formalisation of employee relations in recent years to lengths which may be considered extreme. Although they see themselves as having philosophies in handling employee relations distinctive to their particular enterprises, these are rarely expressed in bureaucratic terms, and rarely supported by comprehensive agreements or documentation. In many cases such an approach would conflict with the sense of independence which individual establishments appear to require. But it would also run counter to the feeling that the business of producing and selling is a practical affair which ought not to be burdened by excessive rigidities of labour administration. It was long ago observed that British employee relations have a preference for procedures and a desire to reduce substantive rules to a minimum. That tradition appears to have been maintained.

Nevertheless, there has been considerable movement from the 'cult of unstructure' which formally characterised the British scene; the 'cult of privacy' has been at least partly breached; and managements, in taking greater initiative, in seeing their role as more 'proactive' and correspondingly less 'reactive' have done something to breach the tradition that everything is negotiable. Although to the outsider it may seem that the pressures stimulating these changes date at least from the National Board for Prices and Incomes and from the Donovan Commission, managements themselves point in the main to the Industrial Relations Act of the Heath government and the Trade Union and Labour Relations and Employment Protection Acts of the Wilson administration which followed. Many of the changes which the survey records have been the result of legislation. The message seems to be clear. Legislation is, from the point of view of moving managements to action, an effective way of ensuring that something is done.

From this description it should be clear that, despite much change, older ways of handling employee relations are still recognisable. The law has not called for standard practice, except by codes and procedures. Nor has it demanded organisational arrangements which would conflict with the variety of approaches which managements prefer. If Donovan has prevailed, this has been in the spirit rather than the letter.

Whether companies would find other, less procedural, interventions by the state so easy to absorb is a different question—if, for example, participatory structures or board arrangements were made compulsory, if mandatory requirements were laid down for trade union recognition, or if wage and earnings arrangements were closely controlled. These do not appear in any case to be questions which the employers in the survey anticipate with any degree of consensus (Appendix 4). Inflexibility and trade unionism continue to concern single establishment companies; no pattern of anticipation of any kind seems to exist in common to multi-establishment concerns. *Obiter dicta* of Lord Palmerston come to mind. Asked if Britain had a foreign policy, he is reported as replying, 'Sir, we have no policy, but our interests are eternal'. This survey suggests that companies will consider the strategy of action if and when the need arises.

The time taken in processing, writing up and publication of the results of this survey has inevitably taken it out of the economic context in which it was conducted. Since the spring of 1980 unemployment has risen from 1.8 million to almost 3 million; redundancies, which were running at about 31,000 a month in early 1980 were reported to be occurring a year later at a rate almost 50 per cent higher than that figure; trade union membership, having risen persistently for the past decade has now begun to fall. For the first time since the war we have been reminded that the conduct of employee relations is a function of the state of demand, trade and employment and that the attitudes and practices built up over the years may fall away as the balance of interest and authority between employers and employees changes from labour to capital. 'I expect', said the writer to one managing director late in 1980, 'that you have been taking advantage of the present situation to reduce your labour force.' 'Yes', he replied, 'I have just got rid of about 300 people whom I have not needed for some time, and without any response from the unions.' I pursued the matter further. 'You will be reducing your personnel staff next.' 'Yes', he said, 'I have already begun.'

It remains to be seen to what extent world recession, followed by governmental attitudes and policy less sympathetic to conciliatory approaches to the demands of employee representatives and more inclined to challenge the assumption of trade union authority, has altered the picture drawn in this survey. Hard data is not easy to find. Personnel posts are more difficult to get and more time is being spent on factory closures than upon recruitment of labour. But are numbers of personnel directors and managers actually falling? A recent survey suggests that this may be so among top companies, that employee relations is regarded by them as of decreasing importance and that the number seeing change as now taking place as a result of pressure from employees is almost insignificant.[1] It is possible that employers are already retreating from the participative, procedural and increasingly professional attitudes to employee relations developed over the past decade. On the other hand, it can be argued that habits, even those built up over a decade only, and even those acquired as a result of often unwelcome legislative and other governmental influence, die hard. British employers are not, by tradition or inclination, quick to take advantage of labour situations. Nor do they usually have any desire to antagonise their labour force more than can be avoided, if only because the future remains unknown. No doubt at some time other academics may be asked to find out the truth of what has begun to happen in the depressed 1980s. At the time of writing it can only be said that we do not know.

1   G. Lindsay Korn/Ferry, Ferry International, 1981, *Boards of Directors Study, 1981.*

APPENDIX 1

THE INITIAL QUESTIONNAIRE

Enquiry into employee relations and decision making

A. Description of organisation

Which of the following most nearly describes your situation in your organisation?   *(Please tick one box only)*

1. **Are you the Headquarters of a Holding Company?** i.e. a company which exercises *financial control only* over its subsidiaries and has no direct production or employee relations function. ☐

2. **Are you the Headquarters or principal company** of a multi-establishment organisation with subsidiaries, groups, divisions, businesses, companies or establishments:—

    (a) which has an employee relations function? ☐

    (b) which has *no* employee relations function? ☐

3. **Are you a group, division, business or company** responsible to the Headquarters of a multi-establishment organisation as described in (2) above? ☐

4. **Are you an individual establishment** or site of a multi-establishment organisation as described in (2) or (3) above? i.e. a separately managed production, construction or trading unit within a multi-establishment organisation. ☐

5. **Are you a single establishment,** public or private company or partnership? i.e. a single production, construction or trading unit managed by a single unified management *not* forming part of a multi-establishment organisation and with *no* subsidiary or associated manufacturing or trading companies or establishments of your own. ☐

If none of these descriptions applies readily to your situation, please explain here

. . . .

. . . .

B. Ownership

Is your company (or in the case of divisions or establishments as (3) and (4) above the company of which you form part)

(please tick one box only)

1. Wholly UK owned? ☐

2. Wholly foreign owned? ☐

3. UK based with (minority foreign interests? ☐
(majority foreign interests? ☐

4. Foreign based with (minority UK interests? ☐
(majority UK interests? ☐

5. 50%–50% UK–Foreign owned ☐

If none of these descriptions applies readily to your situation, please explain here

. . . .

. . . .

. . . .

COMPANY . . . .

Person who completed questionnaire . . . .

Title . . . . Tel.No. . . . .

APPENDIX 2

THE 50 COMPANIES INTERVIEWED

Airtech Ltd.

B.H. Blackwell

Blackwell Scientific

George Bassett Holdings

Bodycote Ltd

British American Cosmetics

British Insulated Callenders Cables

John Brown

Cadec Ltd

Carrington Viyella

Chaucer Press

Cheeseborough

Clarkson Tools

Clay Cross

Coalite

Debenhams

Dickinson Robinson

Dowty

Douglas Holdings

Ford

Gallaghers

GEC

General Foods

Matthew Harvey

Hunt & Broadhurst

Imperial

Independent Broadcasting Association

Healey Mouldings

Hoover Ltd

Kalamazoo

Lindustries

Lucas Industries

Lucy

Massey Ferguson

Metal Box

Henry Mills

Mobil

Montfort

Pedigree Pet Foods

Plessey

Reed International

Rio Tinto Zinc

Shell UK

Siviter Smith

TGM Gauge

Thomson Holidays

Thorn Gas Appliances

Vosper Thorneycroft

N.J. Wild

Wolvercote Mill

APPENDIX 3

MULTI-ESTABLISHMENT COMPANIES:
PHILOSOPHIES OF EMPLOYEE RELATIONS

General philosophical

To engender a group identity as well as a pride in the subsidiary company or division. Good relationships.

To respect the dignity of man. To ensure constant communication both ways. To tackle grievances before they get out of hand.

To encourage a participative, open environment.

People have rights and responsibilities and should be treated fairly and, where possible, generously within overall financial constraints of the business, i.e. paternalistic approach.

Fairness, consideration on both sides, loyalty on both sides.

Do as you would be done by. Try to be scrupulously fair. Try never to change policy.

Maintain integrity of personnel (and other) functions. Ensure frank open debate related to company objectives with responsibility being accepted for actions taken.

All employees are entitled to: a) a fair day's pay; b) security; c) have the right to be heard; d) have the right to know how the business is doing.

Industrial relations

To conform with group employee relations policy as far as possible. To keep within the law, to deal justly with grievances and problems, to participate and communicate freely, to pay fairly.

Orderly and fair dealings with employees having regard to potential, knock-on effects of local actions.

Professional research to determine P & IR positions.

To follow the agreements agreed with management and unions in writing.

Adhere to recognised good personnel practice in order to achieve high performance.

To accept central 'bargaining' for conditions/employment, etc., and to involve staff in participation of the company's business more and more.

238

The company is committed to the principle and practice of equity in reward and consultation with employees in matters which affect their jobs and working environment.

Fair treatment to all employees in line with good UK standards, properly negotiated agreements or legal requirements. Reward and promotion in line with performance.

Full conformity with all legislative requirements. Plant autonomy within broad guidelines. Use of consultative process. Use of national procedures EEF/CSEU.

Cross fertilisation of ideas—group guidelines—a personnel manager's forum meets quarterly.

Ultimately sound industrial relations depends upon strong and purposeful line management working within proper controls, procedures and disciplines. Without pursuing a policy of confrontation, the company recognises its responsibility to initiate and implement change, to exercise and, where necessary, to regain control of the management function.

'Donovanesque':

1   Must conform to local legislation and competitive practice.

2   In certain areas, parent company's philosophies apply, e.g. conflicts of interest, ethical business conduct, incentive payment systems, job evaluation of senior managers, etc.

3   Individual company policies exist on a wide range of topics for company wide application.

To maintain an identity of interest between the company and its employees. To provide for equality of opportunity, for the development of individual ability, and for constructive relations with the recognised trade unions.

Policy rather than philosophy—that good IR are a prerequisite to success.

The company's philosophy is that management has full responsibility for industrial relations matters, and that in order to carry out its management function effectively it needs the practical consetn and co-operation of the workforce.

Employee involvement and hard negotiations.

To be upper quartile performers and remunerators in the appropriate market sector: we encourage involvement; encourage harmonisation; encourage union membership; are decentralised as we believe negotiation takes place where the action is.

Follow established procedures, refer to HQ for guidance.

To maintain good employee and industrial relations through good communications, procedures and agreements with trade unions.

Managerial/man management

The group is beginning to develop a more open, participative style of management, but set against a very traditional background this takes a long time to bear fruit or show results.

To get the best understanding over the complete spectrum of employee requirement, total understanding by senior executive is essential, and thus this knowledge must be the base for industrial relations within the organisation.

Devolved responsibility recognising the need for co-ordination to avoid embarrassing precedents.

Firm, fair and consistent decision making backed by ready access to members of the executive committee. Adherence to agreed company procedures and budgets.

Every manager is responsible all the time. Management includes man management at the top of the list.

Positive clear cut leadership. Respect and mutual interest, i.e. job security, wage growth, etc.

Guided by head office, formally and informally.

Adherence to minimum central conditions, broad principles, etc., but with consideration to local autonomy.

That senior management takes responsibility for IR in conjunction with the group's personnel manager.

Autonomy in most matters—reward for business success but failure held to be responsibility of managing director and his board.

No action should be taken without direct consultation with group.

Manpower organisation

Maximum rates of pay within the capacity of the company to pay a happy and contented staff.

To minimise conflict and to channel aspirations of employees so as to be of mutual benefit.

Good pay and conditions in return for good work and loyalty.

To ensure that the necessary human resources are available, trained, utilised and motivated so as to fulfil the company's long and short term requirements.

This policy will be pursued in such a way as to provide fair rewards for a fair day's work; reasonable working conditions and terms of service; work that satisfies the individual's needs for involvement and the full use of his abilities and skills; and opportunities for advancement and self-realisation. This policy should lead to the employment of the minimum number of people commensurate with the efficient running of the business.

Philosophy involves high degree of employee participation plus high wage/salary and high productivity policies.

To keep employees informed, to involve employees in decisions affecting their employment.

Recognise the importance of employees; consult, involve and participate.

That employees are one of the most important assets and have to be treated as such to secure the company's future as much as investment of capital.

Provide pay at around upper quartile, very good conditions, stable employment and to develop people as we can.

To consider employees as a company asset and to develop and maintain them accordingly.

To establish terms and conditions, either by collective bargaining or otherwise, that enable the company to recruit, train and retrain the high quality of staff necessary for the industry, and to provide as satisfying and rewarding a career as possible in a high technology environment.

Social

To keep units small and to involve staff through formal and informal consultation.

To implement good working conditions (in context of own industry) and encourage maximum co-operation and goodwill between management and workforce at all levels.

Our employee relations philosophy is rooted in that set out in paragraphs 40, 41 and 42 of the Industrial Relations Code of Practice.

To respect, understand and develop the need for harmonious industrial relations through communication, participation and joint consultation.

The Board is concerned for the employee and is always anxious to provide him/her with full employment. It provides a sick scheme and has a contributory pension scheme with widow's pension and death benefit (in service).

Continuity of employment, person to person contact, fair treatment.

A firm management understanding and objective to be fairly reconciled with employee aims.

Treat people decently and 'humanely'. Pay them fairly. Involve them in matters to do with their jobs.

All employees treated the same.

To provide an environment where performance is recognised and rewarded on an equal opportunity basis.

To provide continued and rewarding employment in a climate that encourages all employees to contribute to and share in success.

Disciplinary

Not more than 200 people in one factory. Know all employees—don't let trouble makers start—get rid of them at *any price*—family business— 50 years—never a strike—virtually no industrial action!

Treat them fairly, pay them well and don't stand any nonsense.

Conformity with CIA terms and conditions. Light discipline.

Miscellaneous

Proactive, and consistent across establishments.

Broad policies, guidelines, or specific parameters are issued according to the subject.

Comparability within 'group' guidelines.

Basically we are contractors and that means doing things 'better' than rivals or the client, i.e. the job goes on as far as possible whilst the arguing may continue with settlement backdated.

As expressed in the staff information folder.

ANTICIPATED DEVELOPMENTS IN THE 1980s

Principal subject matter of employee relations in the 1980s
(HQs of multis)

Improving communications systems.
Re-assertion of management initiatives.
Introduction of new technology with lower labour content.
Profit sharing.
Participation and involvement meaningful to the individual employee.
Manning levels.
Communications of business realities.
Pay.
Redundancies.
Hours of work.
White collar unionisation.
More efficient working.
Participation.
Productivity improvements.
Long term decisions as to the form of procedural arrangements.
Harmonisation.
Equal opportunity.
Race relations.
Flexibility of labour.
Improvements in existing productivity scheme.
Introduction of office mechanisation.
Employment policies facilitate change and pay spin off.
Job protection.

Principal structural questions to be determined in 1980s
(HQs of multis)

Right balance between corporate, group, division and plant in responsibilities.
 Staff status.
 None—unless decentralisation leads to problems of comparability/ leapfrogging.

Structure of negotiations.

Interface between non-trade union organised and trade union organised. Whether terms and conditions should continue to be negotiated at national level, the question of pay parity between plants.

Strength and organisation of personnel department. Rationalisation of personnel policy into acquisitions.

Pay.

The organisation of joint (i.e. multi-union) negotiations of common conditions, possibly, but less likely, of pay company wide.

Employee involvement.

Hours of work.

Productivity.

More consultation—open style management, possible organisational changes in order to remain viable in face of foreign competition.

Effect of union amalgamation, i.e. BFAWU and T&G, even greater centralised co-ordination of the determination of terms and conditions of employment.

Decentralising further into smaller self-determining units.

Increase trade union organisation of management grades, employee involvement, communication.

New technology.

Constraints on overtime.

Co-determination.

Economic democracy.

Conditions.

Progressive improvement in management/shop floor communications. Improvement of middle management through training.

Principal anticipated sources of external pressure in the 1980s (HQs of multis)

Trade unions.

Government policies.

Economic (inflation).

Unemployment/job protection.

Effect of high sterling value of company's trading position.

None.

Rate of change and world trading position.

National pay negotiations.

Harmonisation through EEC.

Codes of conduct.

Bad example from elsewhere—particularly public sector.

Pay.

Volume of business.

Move to reduce the working week (work sharing?).

Social and political.

Desire of shop floor for progressive social improvements in line with those obtained (but not earned) by other industries possessing greater trade union muscle despite increasingly difficult situation of our own industry.

Increased competition.

Declining investment.

Recognition claims.

Post entry closed shop.

Principal structural questions to be determined in the 1980s (single establishment companies)

Continue to treat all employees fairly/promote good relations.

Harmonisation. Equal rates throughout.

Trade union recognition.

Shorter working week.

Consideration of staff association if wanted.

The need to give people fancy titles to formalise their responsibilities.

No great change—very little.

None.

Reduction in numbers employed.

Pressure from trade unions for staff status for works employees.

Possible moves toward company wide bargaining for manual workers and non-manual workers together for some issues.

Inflation.

How will greater employee involvement be achieved?

More consultation in company policy and product.

Hope that strikes will be last resort not first for a small company keeping good employees when promotion not possible.

Overformalised, inflexible personnel procedures.

More formal procedures to be introduced.

Retraining.

Introduction of new technology machines and possibly shift work.

Development of management structure that will ensure all grievances are tackled expediently and consistently.

Possible union/non-union conflict within hourly paid staff.

Role of trade union in participation arrangements.

Elimination of all bonus schemes, more attention to man/management, completion of harmonisation process, improvements in communication and employee involvement practices.

More exchange of information.

Automation as alternative to an increased workforce.

As it has always been to strike a fair and acceptable balance between what employees want to 'pick up' and what the company can afford to pay.

New closed shop necessitating more formal and detailed policy for industrial relations.

Wages—incentives related to productivity.

Single status, white/blue collar, voluntary and legal worker representation in larger companies.

Change in attitudes to communication.

More participation in the development of the company.

Principal subject matter of employee relations in the 1980s (single establishment companies)

Profitability and security of employment.

Continue to treat all employees fairly.

Sick pay scheme—perhaps guaranteed week.

Conditions.

Hours of work (shorter week); working life.

Pensions.

Holidays.

Pay (in difficult economic climate); negotiations (of local companies).

None—nothing of significance.

Same as now and a greater involvement in the problems of new technology—this will lead to demands for more holidays and a shorter week.

Financial incentives geared to results.

The problem of existence.

Harmonisation of conditions, manual worker and non-manual worker.

Manning levels.

To get across the message that customers are the ultimate employers and the business exists because we satisfy them; this is essential.

Employee satisfaction is important but secondary and dependent on the former.

Shift differentials and working patterns, hours worked per year.

Problems of change.

How large peripheral benefits (canteen subsidy, pensions, sickness scheme) should apply to employees.

Implementation of job evaluation.

Employee participation.

Further participation in company policy formation and forward planning.

Improvements in pay and productivity, job conditions.

Employee appraisal.

Job protection.

Demarcation.

Greater productivity and job enrichment.

Financial participation.

Status.

Style of man/management.

The opportunity to work.

Job satisfaction.

Principal anticipated sources of external pressures in the 1980s (single establishment companies)

Hard line union negotiations—union pressure for what we cannot afford.

Reflection of union demands. Union interference—excessive influence of trade unions in society at large.

Trade union recognition.

The claim for parity with desirable pay/conditions—an ever widening world exposed by the media, whether we can afford it or not.

The possibility of more 'workers' legislation in the future.

EPA and such idiotic government assistance to workers forcing small company employers with severe threats to continued existence.

Trade union calls for members not involved in a dispute to strike, e.g. employees in private steel plants.

Shortage of business to keep companies going, union pressure for money, etc., with no corresponding commitment. If sales decline this imposes severe constraints, the National Engineering Agreement negotiations create pressures in the domestic situation.

Outside pay rates.

Unemployment.

National pay and wage settlements.

World recession and declining markets.

Mass union seeking procedure agreement with a view to eventual closed shop.

Trade unions, possible trade union activity.

New technology.

Marxism.

Any excessive union demands, inflation and high cost of living, value of pound on Exchange.

Secondary picketing—lack of orders, possible reductions.

Aspirations of a more aware society.

Reduction in working week—earlier retirement.

Wages.

Shortage of skilled labour.

Unreasonable union demands which affect companies not involved in dispute.

Cost of living, inflation.

Government policies.

Sales market.

Labour attitudes.

Possible recession in building industry.

In-house agreements.

Too much legislation which favours the militants.

Well meaning but sometimes ill informed advice from ivory towers— TU, etc.

Trade union officials looking for something to do.

Reluctance to accept foreign machinery, equipment, etc.

Their own domestic problems.

Microchip.

Equal pay.